LOVE IN A PAPER BAG

LOVE IN A PAPER BAG

LEARNING FROM LIFE

JILLIAN RICHARDS

EPIGRAPH BOOKS
RHINEBECK, NEW YORK

Love in a Paper Bag: Learning from Life © 2020 by Jillian Richards

All rights reserved. No part of this book may be used or reproduced in any manner without the consent of the author except in critical articles or reviews. Contact the publisher for information.

Paperback ISBN 978-1-951937-26-3
eBook ISBN 978-1-951937-27-0

Library of Congress Control Number 2020904327

Book design by Colin Rolfe

Epigraph Books
22 East Market Street, Suite 304
Rhinebeck, NY 12572
(845) 876-4861
epigraphps.com

BIRTHING JELLYBEANS

"You should be writing!" became a chorus during the six years I lived in southern California. In a sixth-grade classroom decades before, I had written an essay. The classroom was formal. Well-worn wooden desks stood at attention in rows. Ceramic inkwells into which we dipped our steel-nibbed pens were filled daily. Our teacher forgot and wore her slippers to school one day. This added to the secret joy I took in the fact that her hair was dyed a valiant cobalt blue.

Once a week we read our essays out loud, standing in turn. I do not remember the topic, but I do remember that my very first sentence was read out loud again by the teacher with the cobalt blue hair and then praised by her. The world did not stop spinning, but I remember—still with a smile—the moment when an older, wiser, blue-haired person read words of mine out loud and praised them. "I was wandering aimlessly through the bush," she read. My sentence. My words.

From this vast distance in time I read it again in my mind, and I smile. Whatever led me to such brilliance I do not know, and I certainly do not recall ever having wandered aimlessly anywhere. But I did think for a moment or two back then, that I was so exalted, my inner self would burst right out through the ramparts of my skin. I was ten years old.

I matriculated at the age of sixteen. People told me that was a very young age to matriculate, but I did not know what I could possibly do about that. By the time the results of those important final examinations were published in the newspapers, as was the wont in those days, I was floored into silence to find that I had failed every single subject. It took another twenty-four hours of serious inner denial and chilling stillness, while pretending that I was really not alive, for me to discover that I had been awarded honors! Honors—which were published in a separate section of the newspaper. No older, wiser person had given me this information, and I had not thought to look at the honors list.

Decades later I was invited to work in California. "You are a writer!" my CEO boomed at me during our first meeting in his office. I was stunned. This was a totally unexpected turn in the conversation.

"How could you possibly know that?" I queried. "I have written you a total of one letter and one fax in the past year. All our other communication has been via telephone."

"I am a writer," he boomed, "and it takes a writer to know a writer. And you,"—this with his long bony forefinger pointing hard at me—"are a writer!"

With fifty-two books published, I figured he must have a point.

Life rushed on and I rushed on with it—across California, across the USA, and back and forth to Australia. But something was in the air in that land of opportunity, or in the soup, or in something. Again and again over the six years I was there, the conversation would stop and a firm and determined finger would point directly at me, and a writer of some renown would say, "You should be writing!" It was as though they had conspired to join in an agitated, clamoring but still alien chorus.

But I couldn't summon the energy to write anything down on paper. At the end of each working day, my whole self was too exhausted to even imagine picking up a pencil, let alone attempt to use it. When I eventually discovered a little dictation machine, I dictated wry, Australian-type tongue-in-cheek observations of the plight of man. In airports, between meetings, between courses of dinners and of lunches, in elevators and driving on freeways—I dictated.

Six years on, back in Australia and with more time for myself, I pondered these things and wondered what I would write if I were ever to write it down on paper. No stunning novel was bursting out of me. Neither did I have a palpitating desire to tell the world my life story. What should I write? I cogitated. And I wrote whatever it was that decided to come out of me and find its way onto paper. Out they came—short, tight stories. It was like the birthing of bright little jelly beans.

LOVE IN VARIOUS GUISES

Step-grandmother Isabella from Scotland, who had been married to my Italian grandfather from the island of Corfu, offered love along with salt cod and sago plum pudding. Uncle Percy offered it, wearing a starched apron and holding fresh baked scones in his hands. Auntie Gladys offered it with homemade fruit cake, her singing dog on her lap. Willis offered it with stories. Later, friends offered it in so many generous-hearted ways. But at one profound time in my life it came to me in a paper bag left quietly by the doorway of Nathan's intensive care unit.

LOVE IN A PAPER BAG

Winter brought me the love of my firstborn son.

Spring brought me
the spectacular joy of his growth,
and the charm
of childish bliss.

Summer brought me
the anguish of his life,
too frail to bear
the travails of disease,
in such a minute frame.

Autumn brought me
the poignant love of friends,
to succor,
hold up,
and encourage,
as we wept
through the harrowing days and nights.

Winter brought me small gifts,
blessed gifts
left gently at the hospital door.
Gifts of meals,
offered to nourish my body
and my soul
as I kept vigil
day, after night, after day.

These gifts
brought spring to my heart,
and the sweet possibility of hope.

They were gifts of thoughtful love
proffered in a paper bag.

REVELATION IN A PAPER BAG

In the telephone booth outside the Rhode Island hospital where emergency services had taken my four-year-old firstborn, Nathan David, I stood alone, attempting to call my husband to tell him the news of Nathan's death.

As I stood, great with my third child, I glanced across to the outside wall of that hospital. There hung a huge photograph of a thin young woman holding her severely malnourished child to her breast. They each looked right into my eyes, pleading their desperate cry for help. In that daunting moment of revelation I realized that I was not alone. I was instantly a part of the worldwide community of grieving mothers that arced back through the ages. Boomeranged out of my singular moment of grief and shock, I returned to myself, admonished. It became a moment not just of darkness, but also of enlightenment.

Thus began my next new story, my next new life. Treading gently, I have made my way into each new story of my life. Married and newly single, employed and unemployed, loved and rejected, in birth and in death, in frustration and in fury—I have learned.

THEN

I grew up enthralled by Willis's stories. I came to know his two dogs, Bonnie and Floss, as though they were my own as they raced outdoors with the barefoot Willis at 4:00 a.m. on frosty mornings to rescue the newborn lambs from the crows.

Willis told me about Edward Duer Richards, my paternal grandfather, cutting the home of the Coles family in half after he had negotiated its purchase—and moving it to the family farm in St. James, on the back of a dray, where it was rolled into position over huge hewn logs.

Everyone, and everything, has a story. All that is needed is a gentle poke with—tell me the story of your holiday, or your glasses, or your great aunt—for rivers of amazing stories to tumble out.

Nathan, my spunky little firstborn, loved stories told or read, made-up or true. By the time he was three he liked to take his own little tape recorder and microphone into his bedroom to tell and record his own stories. One of my favorite stories about him comes from the day I was preparing to bring his newly hatched brother Luke Benjamin home from hospital. I thought I had prepared for all contingencies. I strapped Nathan into his car seat and moved to place baby Luke into the car bed. The usually cheerful Nathan looked at his new brother in horror and bellowed, "Get him out of there. That's my bed!"

Nathan David had been named for Nathan the prophet and David the king. Literally, his name meant "beloved gift." Nathan was four years old when he died. There is a lot of story from those years—of hospital and suffering, and of learning the meaning of the word anguish. In this searingly painful time, I was in the midst of a story that was not of my choosing, unprepared. The stories I had told of my life were no longer adequate. I felt stressed, exhausted, and unsure.

Nathan would pray each night, his tiny head bowed and his eyes closed. Serious. Reverent. "Thank You, God, for the day that was the day that we had." Now I attempted to do what Nathan had unknowingly admonished me with as he had prayed. Aware that I could remain stuck, telling the same story again and again, I struggled to grow into a new maturity, a new story.

IN THE BEGINNING

Willis told me that it was extremely hot the day I was born. My mother, however, never spoke of the event. She did not like it, not any of it. The Queen Victoria Hospital, which silently heralded my birth, is now a mere shadow of its former self overwhelmed by upmarket retail stores in a refurbished Melbourne town. And me? I do not remember it at all.

WORLD WAR II

I was a war baby—although the effect on my unformed self of all that death, destruction, fear, and uncertainty did not come to my attention until many decades later. Willis was Air Force, and I grew up with his stories of fighting the Japanese through the jungles of Morotai, Borneo, and Balikpapan. When he returned to us, he and I fought them again, night after night from the side of my bed in East Malvern. The best war stories he ever told me were of his furry war companion, Sid the Monkey, although he also regaled me with tall stories of massive mosquitoes that tramped, army-like, across the chests of the soldiers at night in order to turn over their dog tags and check their blood types before plunging in their proboscises.

Willis, ever the passionate lover of stray dogs and people, held at bay with great difficulty tears of sadness as he remembered his beloved furry companion—but no tears of any kind were shed for the long-legged mosquitoes, tramping in their jungle boots. His stories were repeated endlessly throughout the years of my childhood, and I never tired, not for one instant, of his joy in sharing them over and over. I still treasure a book of small black and white photographs he entrusted me with—photographs of his years in the jungle, of life in a war, which so marked him, and marked me more than I knew.

Three years Willis was gone, into the jungles of war. Merle developed peritonitis somewhere along that war-weary way and was rushed to hospital in the middle of one scary night. It must have been terrifying for her, and it was most certainly seriously scary for my older sister, Anne Miree, and for me—both of us mere babes lost in our own jungle of fear. Merle almost died. Willis was flown home from a jungle filled with mosquitoes and fighting. Not one bit of this can I remember. I was told many years later that Merle draped away six months of recovery time in Nana Richards's home, where my Scottish Auntie Gwen nursed her back to life while also nursing Nana Richards through the spiral to death following a stroke. As a result of Merle's drama, Anne Miree was rushed off into the safety of Nana Richards's home too, while Willis went back to war.

I, however, was rushed off to a Red Cross home. I was one year old. I still remember Willis's eyes opening wide with horror as he and I stood in his garage fifty years on and realized together that I must have stayed in that Red Cross home for up to three years. No wonder I had recurring dreams for decades, of standing in a cot looking through a window across a vast expanse of elegantly manicured green lawn, waiting for I knew not what. I was abandoned and did not know it then, nor for many years. That abandonment echoed through the years of my life, dealt with expertly by a generous dose of denial on my part and silence on the part of most adults I ever encountered. These twin abilities to bury truth in denial and silence led me a merry dance into a life of performance. I became an expert in the art forms of smiling all the time and pushing down painful feelings, particularly the pain of rejection.

"There was no one available to care for you," said Auntie Anne in response to my adult queries about the unspoken mysteries of those days. Her husband, my Uncle Eddie, was a provost marshal in Australia at the time, and landed himself in hospital in Adelaide with a bullet through his buttocks. "In one side and out the other, through the cheeks, you know," he explained to me years later, pointing.

While Eddie was in hospital in Adelaide, Auntie Anne gave birth to two bundles of joy, twin boys, to add to the two toddlers already racing her to early retirement. She was what was called "lying-in" in a Canberra hospital while Uncle Eddie whiled away nine months of his life healing from the bullet wounds in his backside. That was just the way it was. It was wartime, and we were right in the midst of it. Such were some of the unseen sacrifices of a war that stole the life of sixty thousand young Australians. Very much of that war was little spoken of for a long time. So, although I entered adulthood still sorry for the multitudes whose lives had been devastated, I was at the same time unaware of the impact it had had on my life and that of my family. I thought it had missed us.

Willis and his companions knew it did not miss us. From time to time a comrade-in-arms would visit our home, and I glimpsed the warm welcome and the pleasure on Willis's face as he greeted each one. As far as I remember, there was no hugging in greeting or even shaking of hands, but what can only be described as love and respect shone on their faces. They had shared experiences and seen atrocities that no one should ever see in order that I should never have to experience or see them. Once Willis told me a story about the brave man who had just left our house. "His sister was a nurse in Singapore when the Japanese invaded," he told me quietly. "They took her and other Australian nursing sisters down to the ocean, made them face the water, and shot them in the back." That was as much as he could bear to tell me as I watched the retreating back. It left me standing as still as death, tight in the throat with sympathy and wonder. Although he spoke very little of the war, as he grew older and more than slightly senile, Willis would rant, "You would have been a waitress in a Japanese restaurant if it were not for us! I saved you," he was saying. This is why he went. This is why I was left standing up in the cot, searching across the lawn for I knew not what.

Life trudged on like those blood-sucking New Guinea mosquitoes with their hobnailed boots, and people came and went in my life. Some came tramping across my heart with their hobnailed boots, checking my blood type and sucking the life right out of me.

THE BASHER

I can never forget him—a big brash boy. He and his family lived next door to me when I was in infant school. Daily, he would wait for me at that school gate, demanding my colored pencils. In return, he "might" stop his threat to beat me up. The one short block I had to run home from infant school became persecution alley. Of course, I gave him my colored pencils, which left me totally defenseless the next time he accosted me—sweaty, and dirty, and cruel. I had no more colored pencils. The front fence of our modest postwar home was built of brick with a roof-shaped row of shiny clinker bricks capping it. It was at this fence that he leaned in over me, closer and closer. Looming. Breathing rage. Threatening. Terrifying. My sin was that I lived next door. My sin was that I was smaller than he by far. My sin was that I had run out of bargaining tools. My sin was that I was a girl. With no adult in sight to protect me, I ate my fear. I put it down where it could companion the abandonment I must have felt as a babe for all those war years I spent in the Red Cross home.

ICECREAM SUIT

As that war came to an end, Willis was shipped back to Australia, ill. Nine months later he came home to us from hospital bearing gifts he had made during his grueling convalescence. During his recovery he had poured his frustration and patient love into the sewing of matching felt boleros, one each for Anne Miree and for me. They were made from a glorious fuchsia-colored felt, threaded through at the edges with white. Meticulously detailed animals and flowers adorned the fronts. We loved them, and the equally meticulously handmade toy elephant and kangaroo he stitched for us. I wish I had mine still. I had felt his love in it.

He arrived at the door of our home in his ice cream suit. Someone had dressed him up, wound him up, and pointed him in the direction of home. Suddenly, a uniformed stranger was among us. I remember feeling happy, and some rough and tumble and laughter. I do not remember awkwardness or reticence. He just slotted right in. The ice cream suit (or "creams," his Air Force summer uniform) became part of our lives for the next twenty-five years, as he served his country from Point Cook and from the Victoria Barracks. Years later, after watching the terrible unspoken tension between my parents, I asked Willis why he and his ice cream suit had stayed so many years. "I had two little girls," was all he offered. He did not want to abandon us again.

QUEENING AWAY

For the greater part of my life, I have been fascinated with other people's stories. The first person other than Willis whose life grasped my childish attention was the Queen of England,

Elizabeth II. Long before the media tore apart the image of the ideal, the royal family had become a part of my life. They were a part of my heritage, and my sense of belonging was linked to their existence. I was a witting yet unwitting royalist by the time I was five. I read with childish passion the stories of the royal "goings on," grieved with the young princess when her father died, celebrated with her when she was crowned queen and when she married her prince charming, and watched for stories of the birth and development of each of her right-royal children.

Was she perhaps like God? Did she act for God? Did God put her on the throne? Why was she born to be Queen? I liked all the roses and tiaras and crowns and posies. I would like to have been Queen myself. I was sure I could have done all that smiling and waving and general queening that went with the job.

To this day I retain a penchant for a tiara. I once found a copy of an invitation from the 1920s. Printed in bold type at the bottom was *Tiaras may be worn*. That's for me. I will use it one day.

45B BOWEN STREET

Willis had a clinker brick house built on the corner of Fenwick and Bowen streets. He had had the temerity to purchase two blocks of land after his return from the war and enough further temerity to arrange for the blocks to be divided in the opposite direction so that they became two square blocks instead of two long, skinny ones. Hence, they became 45A and 45B. He sold 45A, which then covered his costs for both. Every time he told me that story his chest puffed out a little with his pleasure at doing such a deal.

With no television in 45B and the radio used only for the news, *Billy Bouncer, Dad and Dave*, and *Singers of Renown*—the invasion of my mind and its yet unformed opinions came via the newspaper. I read these while lying on my stomach on the linoleum floor of the kitchen of our three-bedroom bungalow, built in the late-1940s. But the invasion of my mind to beat all newspapers for effect came via that impossibly arrogant influence on the thinking patterns of Australian women, *The Australian Woman's Weekly*.

Our neighbourhood was peppered with boys my age and very few girls. When the weather was warm enough, we played football on the streets. There was no tackling or roughing up, but I do remember my intense sense of self-satisfaction when I learned to dropkick the egg-shaped Australian football correctly.

Willis made me a contraption with which to practise my tennis shots. This involved a clinker brick left over either from the building of our house or stolen from a neighboring one. Attached to this was a long piece of elastic of the type that was used to hold up the bloomers of elderly ladies. Attached to the end of that was a tennis ball. Life on the farm had taught Willis that you could make anything from anything, or fix anything—and he did. We recycled decades before the word became popular.

The dropkick mastery and tennis practice on Fenwick Street led to the need to clean my school shoes. Lying in state on our tiny enclosed back veranda was the only decoration, apart from Penny the dog and a mat on which to wipe our feet. This was our hearty wooden shoe box, built atop four sturdy square legs with a lid that sloped towards you. The brass knob to pull up the lid was well-polished, and pulling it revealed a plethora of accoutrements for the cleaning and polishing of shoes. Willis taught me all I ever needed to know about this art in case I too decided to join the Forces and would require the parade gloss he loved so. Balancing on one leg with the other leg lifted so that the shoe rested on the sloping lid, daubing on Kiwi polish with a black bristle brush, and ultimately rubbing with softer and softer cloths—led to the drama of trying to see yourself in the resultant glow. It became a daily ritual for him and for me. In those days the school shoes were the only ones I had, and woe betide me if I had the effrontery to grow out of them. Willis, I believe, is otherwise occupied these days, but I do wish I had kept that green-painted shoebox.

Books did not abound in our house, and I retain no dog-eared copies of childhood books I adored. Nevertheless, I have fond memories of reading, tucked cosily in under the bedcovers. The one and only bookcase we owned was built-in, a novel and extravagant feature. That bookcase, containing our family library, was built to the right of the living room fireplace and consisted of three shelves filled with books that did not move on or off the shelves very often. I remember a period of earnest research into our brown-covered volume of *The Universal*

Home Doctor: Illustrated during my adolescence since any attempt at sex education was entirely missed or considered entirely unnecessary by both Willis and Merle. *The Universal Home Doctor: Illustrated* did not help me very much.

I inherited the books from that daring little library. They included a series of cumbersome brown volumes such as, *The New Standard Illustrated Dictionary: How It Works and How It's Done*, and *The Atlas*, as well as small, intense diatribes on topics such as, *The Cross and the Blood* by J. N. D. In those days, in our particular church it was considered an act of outrageous arrogance to print the full name of the author anywhere in the book he had written. But J. N. Darby was revered as next to God by certain male members of the church, so his name was certainly known and spoken of with awe. Where he lived and died, I do not know, although I believe it was somewhere in "the Old Country," as England was known. How he gained a following of devoted, unquestioning men, I do not know either. Perhaps he had learned that a little mystery could produce a panting following such as is seen still in some religious gatherings. I do not remember that he had a matching following of devoted, unquestioning, or panting women.

THEY HAVE TO GO NOW

For many years and across many oceans I carried dozens of the small, beautifully bound volumes of diatribes by this man. They had a seriously academic look when sitting on a bookshelf and felt like a little bit of home when I was living so far from home. But one year, they suddenly took on the feeling of a tightening noose. They were no longer a comfort. Now they were a burden. I offered them to friends, but no one I knew needed them, so I bundled them up and took them to the local thrift shop, leaving quickly in case they placed them back in my hands.

BRETHREN

We in that church were known as the brethren—brethren being carefully spelled with a small *b*. The reason, I was told, was that we were a simple band of brothers. What happened to the simple band of sisters? Were they to be a panting following of the brothers? By the time I was five I had learned that we were not a sect or a system—or heaven help us, a denomination. We were to expect ridicule and rejection. I did not like that at all. I had also learned that I was a girl, and girls were not allowed to ask questions, let alone think or have an idea. There was a serious absence of discussion, much denial, and a group of folks surrounding me who would rarely acknowledge a weakness or a feeling. I was and am a product of such, although now learning slowly to be less mummified.

Those many of us from the brethren who have maintained relationships throughout the vicissitudes of our lives call ourselves The Featheries with a wry smile. "Really screwed us up," some have said.

FEATHERIES

You know how it is.
Birds of a feather flock together.
Who outside ever could
Or ever would,
Understand us?
Who outside could ever imagine
The communion of friends,
Insulated and isolated
From the world
By religious creed,
And dogma.
We were taught that we had a hold
On the truth.
Self-righteousness
Was spooned down our throats
With mother's milk.
They, the other,
Were our foes.
Still today we hear the railing
Of the orthodox,
Jews,
Christians,
Muslims.
Know-it-alls.
The arrogant.
Those who judge out of fear.

Those who judge without mercy.
Those who judge out of ignorance.
Those who judge too quickly,
And from a hardened heart.
Those who enjoy the power of bullying.
Those who crow with unjustified hate.
Those who have never lived
In the imprisonment of mind
We have known,
But have lived
In an imprisonment
Of their own making.
And so
We step gently towards each other,
Asking,
Not telling.
Listening,
Not speaking.
Watching, with patient heart.
Waiting, with open mind.
We step, with prudence.
We step, where it is safe.
We open our eyes
To complexity.
We open our eyes
To complication.
We open our eyes
To the need for forgiveness.

Or the withholding of forgiveness.
We seek wisdom.
We seek maturity.
We allow time.
We know the possibility
Of misinterpretation.
As we search for simpler answers
In the paradoxes of life.
We deal with the mirror.
And we know how long
It has taken us,
To come
This far.

No flowers decorated our church, and neither organ nor piano were allowed for many of the years I attended. I was told that such frivolities would distract us from our worship of God. Confused puzzling teased at my mind, as I had thought that God made flowers and that He loved music. One assigned elder had the supreme honor of using the tuning fork to set us off on the right track with our hymn singing. I did not think the tuning fork was considered holy but wondered who made the decision that he could be the one to use it. No woman I knew ever touched it.

There was no dancing allowed either, and no movie-going or theatre-going or ice skating or tap-dancing lessons or ballet. We did not visit art galleries. The young ones joked together that the elders believed that dancing would lead to sex. They must have been trying to keep us as white as the driven snow. Either they did believe that as truth, or they were not aware of the frantic groping and petting by the teenagers in the backs of cars.

SCHOOLGIRL FEELINGS

A small group of us senior girls stood mute on the MacRobertson Girls' High School assembly hall balcony, looking down at the gently moving mass of all the other seniors learning ballroom dancing. They were being prepared for the end of year formal. Boys, pimpled and sweaty, had been brought across from our brother school, Melbourne Boys' High. Resplendent in our school uniforms, we stood above them, a glum little group, and there was not much talking. Standing apart from me, the others were all from the exclusive brethren, whose demands were even stricter than those of the brethren group to which I belonged.

Not knowing names for feelings other than happy, sad, and angry, I did not breathe in and out very much up there on that balcony. My breath was held down inside me, buried deep along with my feelings.

I longed to dance. Music wanted to expand into my body and move me along with its joy. I wanted to be unafraid, but it seemed like rebellion. I was dunked deep into the oil of conformity and obedience. It stuck all over my feathers and glued my feet to the ground. Conflict between what I desired and what I was allowed offered no light-hearted solution. I must have been frustrated, angry, and confused, but I was not yet moved to action.

I had not yet met Frank. I had not watched him bend gently forward as he admonished me, "Up until now, do you know what a triangulated relationship is, Jillian?" he asked. I did not. "It is God and the man against you, and you cannot win." I felt myself slammed against the back wall. He was giving me names for feelings, permission, and revelation. I would begin to poke my nose out of this paper bag and breathe fresher, healthier air.

ON MY FEET, DANCING

Years later I was reveling in the joys of cruising when I spied a gray-haired gentleman. With his back to me, he sat at the bar until the band started into the rhythm of Cuban music. I had been told that he was over eighty and that his wife had died some years before. He continued to cruise, alone. Daily he came to the open deck around the pool where the adventurous frolicked and the air was filled with the smell of good food. He slid from the barstool to his feet, unable to sit still. Alone with his joy, he gave way. I could have watched him for hours. I reminded myself that when I am in heaven, I will be on my feet dancing.

Griff could dance, and with him, I could too. He was light on his feet. With him I did not need to try. "Just walk with me," he said. Now I watched an eighty-year-old man dancing alone, his face shining with bliss. He was not performing for us. Perhaps he was dancing again with his wife. I watched, entranced. I could hardly bear all that beauty and music. I moved towards him, grinning my gratitude. He beckoned. And we danced. And I could. And I did.

LOVE IN THE LIVING ROOM

On the opposite side of our fireplace in 45B was a built-in wood box, a novelty and considered modern. It was painted in a soft eggshell green. Merle liked the color. In the front of the wood box, a door which opened downwards hid the chopped wood from view, especially from visitors and especially from the Queen—should she come to visit, which I fully expected she might do. Wood was delivered by truck to our backyard where Willis split it, log by log. From him I learned how and where to swing an axe for full and easy effect by the time I was six. I also learned where not to swing an axe by the time I was ten, with the permanently split toenail on Willis's right big toe as a constant gruesome reminder of cause and effect.

The wood box had two exciting features. At the back, hidden from living-room view, was a secret opening to the outside of the house. There, the cut wood could be loaded into the wood box without having to be carried across the precious, pure-wool, Axminster carpet that graced the floor. This was a most confrontingly ugly carpet. We walked daily across its huge open poppies as they stared at us and blinked. They were very hard to miss. *Pure wool*, I was to be told more times than

I can count. Willis loved it with a passion it until the day he died. His coffin was carried out across its threadbare remains.

IN A KITCHEN DRAWER

Except for Japanese standards, the kitchen of 45B was small. It had a small built in nook (or eating area). This contraption consisted of a table to seat four with a wooden bench built along each side. The long seat of each bench was lidded, and when raised revealed Willis's collection of newspapers, stacked in piles as high as the Empire State Building. The table was covered with linoleum to match the floor and banded all around with metal.

Each meal time I slid in along the bench first, followed by Merle. Opposite me Anne Miree slid in, followed by Willis. This ritual never changed in all the years we lived there. At the end of each meal I disappeared under the table and scooted out around various feet, only to reappear whole and unharmed in the space between the table and the refrigerator.

The sink area was flanked by two small drawers. To the left, the drawer contained a selection of mesmerizingly boring bone-handled cutlery. *The silver* was preserved for Sunday use only and only in the dining room. The drawer to the right of the sink held the history of Willis's lunch preparations. Merle never appeared for breakfast, so Willis was on duty every day. I do think now that Merle must have been permanently depressed, although I never did hear that word in my youth. I suspect Willis's frustration bubbled beneath the surface, but he kept it from us.

Into this cauldron of frustration and depression Willis threw his creative self, eking the daily rations into paper bags full of lunch for Anne Miree and me, as well as for himself. The offerings were usually a sandwich and a piece of fruit. We had no store-bought treats to enliven those years of soggy tomato sandwiches and squashed banana, which left our leather school satchels permeated with the dead banana odor that ex-pat Australians laugh about together to this day.

Dinner was always at six, with Willis arriving back from the barracks at five thirty in time to change out of his uniform into "civvies," and come into the kitchen for his daily ritual of wiping down the greaseproof paper he had wrapped his sandwich in that morning. Next, he would shake out the paper bag, wipe it with a dry cloth, and check it for greasy spots. If it only had one or two, he would flatten it as lovingly as if he were preparing to wrap a gift. Both greaseproof paper and paper bag were then placed into the right-hand drawer, which also held the family collection of pencils and an assortment of rubber bands. It is beyond me to imagine how many times Willis used and reused the paper bags, but one way or another, despite the soggy sandwiches and squashed bananas, I remember lunch as love in a paper bag.

We had a dog. Always had a dog. We also had a cat for what seemed like a short period of time. We had a budgerigar too. But for one period of my childhood I kept a mouse. It was a cute, waffly-nosed little creature, much prone to escape and exploration. It once found its way to Willis's paper bag drawer, where it made a bit of a mousy mess. Duly admonished, it was put back where it belonged. But English was not its second language, and with freedom on its mind it scurried in a determined way back to the paper bag drawer, where it birthed several small mouselings. Now we had tiny pink jelly-bean-shaped mice in a paper bag.

BRETHREN KIDS

There was a boy called Trevor who hung about with the brethren kids. Trevor and I were once alone. I was thirteen, he fourteen. I remember not why I was there. But I do remember that he was ranting at the time, wishing that his mother would hear yet hoping she would not, with all the arrogance of a fourteen-year-old. He wanted her take the *rotten thing* away from his field of vision and out of his sight. It was an embarrassing offense to him. The "rotten thing," which sat right in front of our knees, was a piecrust coffee table.

His father had worked hard and provided well for the family. He was respected in his field. His mother had spent of the earnings with the care that is the wont of a true Scottish woman. The living room furniture all had a well-bred look, and it was this furniture that he and I were discussing.

Just emerging from childhood, his opinions were spilled all over me, his only audience that day. He told me that he could never bring these thoughts into the family dinner table conversation, but there was a slim chance that I might understand his anger at the ugliness of it all.

In his opinion, the edge of the coffee table brooked no competitors. Its offense was that it was fluted like the flouncing edge of a southern belle's prom dress. For better or for worse, it was called a piecrust edge. As it sat right there in front of us in the stippled light of the afternoon sun, it shamed and offended him—he with a sensitivity to design that would ultimately grow into an ability to manage a firm with dozens of architects. Dust motes, disturbed by his anger, hovered and shimmered anxiously like flightless birds. But he was so certain of his views and so wonderfully self-righteous, that I dared not speak—although mentally, I remained staunchly defensive of his mother's freedom to choose whatever she wished to have in her own living room. My mind hovered and shimmered uncertainly like the dust motes.

Any real piecrust I had seen had not had the temerity to announce itself with such an edge. Piecrusts in my household were edged with straight, fork-tine-marked edges, all lined up like the thin lips of maiden aunts. None were as flamboyant or rambunctious as this table's edge. How could I have known that, years later, this eagerly and contemptuously expressive student would call to invite me out on one of the very few dates of my youth—and then, to flaunt it all again, have the audacity to wear on that date *blue suede shoes*?

On that long past afternoon, his creative spirit was reaching far beyond the edges of the offensive table to a place where objects of desire would be designed, not decorated. Stripped down they would be—clean of decorative despair, essential in their beauty, heady with pure form. He was already hopelessly and irretrievably lost to the need for anxiety-free artistic expression. I, on the other hand, was speechless.

Time tracked its weary way through the weeks and months of my student life until I stood, tremulous, at the edge of a maiden's life—all sixteen years of it—thin, lacking in worldly wisdom, gauche, and unsophisticated in the extreme when he called. For me.

It was eons before the brilliant invention of light-footed communication by means of the mobile phone when his call came ringing from the living room of the piecrust coffee table right into the living room of 45B. There, our one and only black handset resided atop a hand-crocheted doily, atop the eggshell colored bookcase in view of every member of my family. It sat like an offering on an altar in obeisance to the dawn of modernism and the post-World War II era. With the bookcase, the wood box, the pure wool carpet, and the telephone—we had reached new heights of post-WW II sophistication. But that sophistication definitely did not include me. That the telephone rang was a rare enough occurrence. My family watched and waited. Secrets were not safely shared via telephone. The crossing of our pure wool, loudly floral carpet is printed permanently into my mind—seared with marks as clear as those of a hot jaffle iron on bread.

TOOTGAROOK, LAND OF THE CROAKING FROG

Willis purchased a mean little lot of bracken-covered sandy soil in Tootgarook on the Mornington Peninsula after he returned from three years of fighting during the Second World War. On this unlikely plot he built our family beach house. Our chalet. In retrospect, it was a two-room shack, but we loved it, and I spent galloping hours with sunshine and waves, seashells and kelp, friends and cricket on the beach, bore water and rabbit traps.

Willis reminded us to "watch out" when we went wandering off. Watch out for mine shafts. Watch out for snakes. Watch out for redback spiders. During my wanderings, from time to time I came across a narrow mine shaft with its slurpy-looking water staring back at me with baleful eye from far down toward middle earth, toward China, which I believed was down there somewhere. Under Willis's tutelage I learned to set and release rabbit traps. I learned to spear fish at night. I learned how to drop a bore. I learned the taste of brackish water. And I learned to hide outside when Willis went through the nightly ritual of lighting the incandescent ceiling lamps, which burst into glory with a puff and a flare. On the other hand, if I came across an evil-looking snake on the way through the straggling bracken to collect a billy full of milk from the corner store, I had been taught to jump over it and run for my life, never looking back. A billy is what we Australians call a campfire canteen and is famously sung about in "Waltzing Matilda."

The local beach had a dramatic set of side-by-side swings. Industrial strength chains hung down from a heavy metal frame, holding wooden plank-like seats. I loved these swings with a girlish passion. A wild child arrived one fine day while I was swinging ever upwards toward the sky. His evil eye filled with spite. I could smell the danger, but I could not quickly come back to earth from my place in the sky. His swing was let go with a maniacal yell and flew towards me in a menacing arc. I braced my girlish body and ducked, but the back of my skull bears a hard, little bump to this day. It is a wonder I was not ruined for life.

PADDLING MY CANOE

School. The brethren. Camps. Gymnastics. Church. Tootgarook. Friends. Aussie-rules football on Fenwick Street. High School. College. And suddenly, one bright day I was married. A new life. Then twenty-seven years on and just as suddenly, one not-so-bright day I was divorced and shot full pelt into the middle of another new life—the life of the suddenly single. No training had ever prepared me for this life. All of Willis's stories, even of war, left me with neither a rudder nor a paddle for my new canoe. There it all was—my birth, World War II, the Red Cross home, the brethren and J. N. D., the Queen, school, college, marriage, the birth of three beloved children and death of one, and sudden death by divorce.

DREAMS IN A PAPER BAG

An image in my mind has all the bright clarity and innocence of any in a child's picture book. I see a cottage. The blue door is dead center, sporting a shiny brass handle. Windows each side are draped with curtains drawn across softly like a pair of fluffy aprons. In front of a white picket fence and exactly in front of the gate stand a family of four—father, mother, one boy child, and one girl child. Geraniums and daisies splash bursts of color through the palings. A small dog, ears pricked in anticipation, sits by the boy. A small cat, ears pricked and tail curled, sits by the girl. Behind the family the sky is blue, blooming with cumulus clouds. The sun sits to attention at the horizon, a bright orb of glory. Its rays glow off to all corners of the universe, jubilant. This is the way I imagined family. I drew that scene more than once, coloring with joy, loving particularly the benevolent sun.

Knowing little of the inner workings of friends' families, it seemed that I idealized them. Some did look neater, more orderly, more serene, more pleasing, and more comfortable than mine. More pleasing to my eye. Thus, it was that I walked on, blinded by that idealization with its burnished rays, knowing nothing. In the way of a twenty-two-year-old, I married a man I believed loved me. He was smarter than me, better educated than me, better looking than me, and far more godly than me. He told me so. And I believed him.

It took me years to step off the page of the childish picture-book images and contend with the forces of reality. In the twenty-seven years of that marriage I experienced anguished bewilderment again and again. Anything I attempted to confront led to me being told to get down on my knees and beg forgiveness. And I did. We had planned one year in the US for him to pursue his dreams of further studies in Bible. The planned one year turned into ten as he grew to love the academic world and his success in it far more than he had ever loved me. Everything that was wrong was my fault. Again and again, I was expected to work one more year while he studied for one more degree. And I did. We moved from one lot of rented accommodations to another as my longing for a nest grew. We moved from Vancouver to Chicago; to Sydney; back to Chicago; to Beverly Farms, Massachusetts; and to Salem, Massachusetts; to Providence, Rhode Island; and to Fall River, Massachusetts.

While in Salem I gave birth to Nathan and was only able to work part-time. With Nathan's illness and the subsequent births of Luke Benjamin and Toby John, my husband finally had to work full time. He punished me. By then we had been married nine years.

Each time I raised the question of a home of our own, I was told God would give us a house.

We returned to Australia for him to continue his studies on scholarship for a PhD in history. But something went wrong along the way so that when we stood on the doorstep of the college in Sydney—me with nine-month-old Toby in my arms and three-year-old Luke by the hand, preparing to be received with open arms—we were met by a gentleman who summarily informed us that the promised accommodation was no longer available. We were not even invited inside. It was stupefying. We had packed all our worldly goods and traveled across the US and the Pacific Ocean for this? Long-suffering distant relatives took us in for many weeks until we found rented accommodation and I found work one more time.

The next year was a blurred round of rising at 5:30 a.m. to prepare for the day—hanging out the washing, feeding all, dropping the boys at a baby-sitter's, working all day, picking up the boys, bringing in the washing, preparing and cleaning up dinner. My only respite was the thirty minutes I lay on the floor before dinner, too exhausted to move, while the boys giggled and squealed as they climbed and crawled all over me.

I was done. It was his study or the marriage. I had nowhere to go, but I was going. I was desperate.

And so he went to work, and so he punished me. For years. And God *did* give us a house. And his name was Willis. "It's your turn now," he said as he gave me the deposit. He had not spoken of what he saw. But he saw.

There was never to be the family I perceived in my childish imagination. Not the cottage. Not the picket fence. Not any of it. What I was living in was not even close.

Was it a dream? A fantasy? Was it a delusion? Was it hope? Was it ignorance and stupidity? Was it all of these? All these were slowly being squeezed out of the paper bag of dreams I had carried close to my heart—and into the light of truth and its consequences.

DIVORCE

It was unthinkable that the word should be spoken. In our family and in our church—to cover over, repress, and deny a thousand sins was better than to risk such a resolution. But Willis had died and Merle had died, and they were never to know. Merle had stepped so far back into her second childhood by the time Willis died that she tried to have him buried in the oldest pair of pants and work shirt she could find. She was saving money, or so she thought. Rather than confronting her, I was forced to creep into his bedroom, invade his wardrobe, and run like mad out the back door to the car of the mortician with Willis's best suit in hand. I do think he looked much better in the suit than he would have in the old pants and work shirt—more dignified at least, although he did love those old pants and shirt. I resisted the urge to pin his war medals to his chest.

Merle died exactly two years later to the day. The mortician told me that was not unusual. He had seen even odder things. But it spooked me out. There certainly had been no appearance of a loving, tightly bonded relationship between the two of them, so why this clinging in death?

But I was divorced and well and truly what Willis used to call, "up to the front of the line." I was up to the front of a whole new life. And then, after six years of living and working in southern California, and with my trusty E420 Mercedes pointed towards the sun, I was up to the front of yet another new life. I was about to emerge from the southern California sunshine into another set of life's offerings. On this new journey I was going to leave the West Coast and drive alone across the whole big, wide country of the United States to live in Destin, Florida. Friends who were mildly mystified and moderately concerned about me attempted to offer their encouragement by telling me that they did a similar thing once. Each one had a slightly pitying, slightly alarmed look. Later, each of them told me that they were twenty years old at the time, or that they did not really travel alone at all. Not a one indicated that they wished they had the courage to do what I was planning. They each had the appearance of backing slightly away from me as they said goodbye.

ADVENTURE IN A PAPER BAG

Exhilaration was sealed in with me as I set sail in my trusty Merc. As I planned my journey I had cogitated about my car. Should I sell it? Should I ship it to Florida? Should I fly across country? What about a train journey? Then with a thunder of horror, small planes flew through the twin towers in New York City, and my decision was made. I would drive.

Casey had offered me her home as a haven for the weeks between the sale of my home and my departure from California. I waved her goodbye as I drove away, off into another new life. "Be not afraid," was my mantra. Over and over I reminded myself, *Be not afraid*. It was both an admonishment to me and a prayer to God. "You have to look after me," I told Him in no uncertain terms. "You promised, so You have to keep Your promise. I have no father, no brother, no husband. My boys are across the Pacific in Australia. I have been turfed out of the job for which I left Australia. You *have to* look after me." I put a lot of emphasis on the "have."

I was not going to be stuck, or daunted, or frightened. I did not want the self-pity I had learned to stand up against. In California I had learned that I could do anything, take on any task. Australian friends who had visited remarked that I had become again the person they had known when we were teenagers. I hit the road feeling the freedom of my little red scooter. All was in front of me: new home, new friends, new job, new opportunities, new challenges, new dreams, renewed hope.

I journeyed through low desert and high desert, day and night, wet and dry, known and unknown. I visited family and friends, gas stations and cafes—as I moved towards Destin, Florida.

If I had known at nineteen what I knew as I sat inside my Mercedes cocoon, how much more wisely I might have chosen my path or responded to those who crossed my path. But as Frank had said to me in his gracious way, "Up until now." I had learned a lot—yet at the same time had everything to learn. Turfed out of my nest one more time, I had popped out of the paper bag of security where I thought I knew what was next into the rarefied atmosphere of insecurity where I could not see over the horizon. I was inside a paper bag of adventure, peeping out into the future, waiting for it to open up for me.

The paper bag of my life had continued to open, popping or thrusting me on into another new space—enlarging, enlightening, encircling, and ultimately catapulting me into larger and less confined worlds of mind, body, and spirit. The hopes in me were encouraged by Griff's offer of a safe haven. The dreams of my future were not yet birthed. The experiences of my life were tucked beneath my wings, fueling me forward on this adventure in a Mercedes paper bag.

ALWAYS HAVE LACE ON YOUR PETTICOAT

A few weeks into my working life in California, Casey invited a few friends to her home to meet me. They were a sweet bunch of women, and I was grateful for Casey's kindness. She followed up on our relationship, and I met her husband and two daughters. They shared their home with big open hearts. I asked Casey later why she had pursued our relationship. "When you crossed your legs at that first afternoon tea," she told me, "the edge of your petticoat showed. It was a black petticoat with a cream lace border. I thought that anyone who would wear a petticoat like that must be interesting."

I wish I had kept it.

CALIFORNIA GIRLS

Elizabeth did not miss a beat. She carried herself like an expensive and stately African princess, particularly when her hair was braided intimately close to her head, as finely wrought as good metal work, in cornrow braids. Her smile lit up the room.

Her bearing exuded confidence. Her awareness of the world caused her eyes to sparkle with humor. I asked her to work with me after seeing her only once, walking down a corridor. It was the way she walked. I took the risk. I asked her. She took the risk. She agreed. Elizabeth became my executive assistant, and I was blessed.

I reported to a man who had invited me to move from Sydney to California to work with him for the next ten years, after one meeting. He took the risk when he offered, "Tell me what your gifts are, and let's work with them."

I took the risk and said, "Okay." So this newly single woman packed up and moved herself right across the Pacific.

Very newly in California and very early one morning, my telephone jangled as if from the other side of the earth, impatient for my hand to move towards it. Impatient as a hungry child. Complaining. Relentless. Demanding my undivided attention. A deep burrow of sleep still enfolded me. Reluctance was my master. Inertia was my partner in crime. But jangle it did, its continuing savage determination pounding at my ear, my dreams, my comforting rest.

At five thirty in the morning I was in no shape for conversation. At five thirty in the morning I was in no shape for anything except returning to the blissful cocoon of my sleep. But the impatient child would not be quieted. At the other end of the line the disembodied voice sounded vaguely familiar. A male. Older. Gravelly-voiced. Concerned. Concerned? Why? Now I was awake. Now I was listening. Now I was present in the world of sights and sounds and smells—all suddenly bright and sharp, and clear and in focus. "I am sorry to call you so early in the morning." I was trying to still my heart. My heart told me it was not going to be a good surprise. It wasn't. "There's been a fire at your house."

For some months I had lived in a delightful California cottage. Close to my place of business, it had become my haven. My nest. But, as is the way of life in a nest, I was turfed out. Turfed out and not even sure I had fledged. My nest was to be demolished to make way for a parking lot. I would need a new nest. On the salt-washed coast of sunny Sydney stood my other home. A sentinel. A beacon. My mortgaged security. I had purchased that home while driving my car on the freeways of southern California at midnight at the end of a very busy day. The good friend on the other end of the telephone in Australia, appointed to negotiate for me at the auction, rattled me with, "I only offered twenty thousand dollars more than you said to offer. You won't be sorry." Only twenty thousand more? Of my money, not his. Buying from an unforgiving distance had been enough of a risk. And twenty thousand more? My risk. Not his. "But a rainbow came out over the harbor at the end of the auction," he said, as though that justified his action. Maybe it did.

I had hunted up a second nest in California. It was all a bit much for a single girl in a foreign land. They told me with great sincerity and even greater conviction that, until I had stepped ashore in the US, I absolutely had not existed. The bank told me so. Nothing I could produce—neither birth certificate nor driver's license, nor share portfolio, nor letters of introduction—would convince them that I had any life prior to my first two years in California. I was single—and a woman, to boot. Where was the *man* whom they expected to be available to sign papers? I had checked under the bed that very morning, and he was nowhere to be seen. So no loan. And it could well have been no home but for another of this world's blessed risk-takers. A woman, a bank manager, and a risk-taker. How wonderful.

So, with much risk-taking on her part and much more risk-taking on my part, I bought me a second house. With a mortgage. And now there was a fire? I had not even moved in yet. And there was a fire? I had signed the papers only two days ago. And there was a fire?

I was Elizabeth's role model. She told me so. Properties on two continents. She thought that was definitely a thing a girl could aspire to. But there was a fire. "The fire engines have been and gone," he said. "I had a call from the neighbors," he said. "They did not know who had purchased the house, so they called me. I will get dressed and meet you there." Thirty-nine years he had lived in that house before I bought it.

The air was filled with the acrid smell of smoke as I turned into the cul-de-sac which nurtured my new home. As I stepped out of my car a blue-robed angel neighbor walked towards me out of the mist of a pale California morning. Shrouded she was, in both mist and a pale blue dressing gown. I did not know her, but I put my head on her shoulder and wept.

Her story went like this. "I never sleep with my windows open, but I did last night. I was woken by a beeping. I got up and searched our house. Oven timer. Smoke alarm. Telephone. Computer. Nothing. So I went outside and followed the sound down the street. There was nothing to be seen, just disembodied beeping. It drew me towards the big front window of your house," she said. "I peered through, and inside it was all white. Just smoke, smoke and more smoke. It smelled full of dread."

She called the fire department. Then she called the previous owner. Then he called me. And here we all were, at five-fifty in the morning.

The fire department had sent four of their big ladder trucks. Four? In our little eight-house cul-de-sac? Quite a house-warming party, I thought, for my poor little nest. A can of wood filler had been left on top of an oily rag by a careless painter. "Spontaneous combustion," the fire chief told me later. "Very common. Two minutes later and the whole house would have gone up. You were lucky."

Risk and chance in a foreign land.

A QUIVER FULL

I loved to visit Papa Abdullah's restaurant when I lived in Orange County. There was something about eating at Papa Abdullah's. It may be Papa Abdullah's son, who took over after Papa's twenty years in charge—his incredible smile, his sweet spirit, his genuine interest in life, and the love that he poured into the food he prepared. "I am Abdullah," he would say. Courtly. Courteous. Considerate. Caring for our needs with the grace of a ballet dancer.

Or maybe it was the way he took me to his kitchen and pointed to one tired and lonely post card clinging to the wall, bravely hailing "Australia," sent to him by one of his Lebanese relatives. Or maybe it was the way he told me every time I visited that, in Australia, he had a multitude of relatives. And we smiled and nodded and agreed that Australia is indeed an amazing and wonderful place—and that one day he should and must visit. Or maybe it was the food he prepared, so succulent and fresh that I was nourished by the sheer thought of it. Or the coffee he offered, gentling my mind with his conviction and certainty of purpose. Coffee requires thoughtful preparation to taste as you like it. "Would you like to see?" he asked. I would like. Sugar syrup is heated slowly, just past a gentle simmer. The beans, imported from Lebanon, are different in their aroma and in the majesty of their taste. They inspire indolence, refreshment of mind and body, relaxation, ease of spirit. How many times I savoured their fragrance and relaxed into their sweet breath.

Abdullah's clients shared in the bliss. His coffee spoke of deep conversation, longing for home, moments to be remembered.

Or maybe it was the driving around the city circle one more time, past the dusty plethora of antique shops and the manicured officialdom of Chapman University until I finally parked as close as I could to Papa Abdullah's. Once a family home, it stood with a restaurant room lurching against one side like a lost lover. It was neither trendy nor glamorous, yet I was attracted there again and again like a fly to flypaper.

I went there by myself and felt at ease eating alone, drinking Lebanese wine. I went there with friends from California and across the United States, and I took almost every friend who arrived from overseas to eat with me, to fellowship. On my last visit I took with me two women friends to share the lunch hour. One, great with child, was due to deliver herself of a second babe in a month. So, as is the wont with women who have birthed a few bairns of their own, the talk turned to babies—ours, theirs, and of course his—Abdullah's. We asked him, this shy Adonis, this provider of all good things to feed both body and soul, "Do you have children?"

Out of the corner of my eye I saw him move. I was snatched to attention by the straightening of the broad back, the sparkling of the blackest of eyes, and the sheer grace of the swift turn towards us.

"Oh yes," he giggled, "we did four!"

COOKING IN A G-STRING

After the telephone call telling me of the fire in my new home, I was roused from my slumbers quick time a few weeks later at 6:30 a.m. More trouble?

It was my son Toby, calling from Sydney. "The main reason for my call Mum ..." he started in. My mind was racing. "The main reason for my call Mum, is .... What is 350 degrees Fahrenheit in Celsius?" I waited. "I want to cook Lemon Delicious, and I don't know what 350 degrees Fahrenheit means." I laughed with relief. It was midnight in Australia, and his mouth was watering for the comfort food of Lemon Delicious, a family favorite.

FOOTPRINT PIE

Our sweet family favorite of all time was Footprint Pie.

Friend Diane, mother of six, shared the recipe. My boys loved it. When Diane was ill, I suggested we take some food to her family. The boys agreed. "Footprint Pie," they suggested. Despite the fact that this was her recipe, they insisted. I baked. They helped. Into the little brown car we climbed. The pie was placed, *just so* on the floor. Careful instructions were given about the placement of small feet. We arrived at Diane's all excited, and Toby stood up, right onto the pie. Voila! Footprint pie. And so it has been ever since.

> Cream 500 gr butter with 1 cup sugar.
> Beat 1 egg with 1/2 cup milk, and add to mix.
> Stir in 2 cups SR flour until you can pick it all up and roll it in your hand.
> Press into pie dish and bake for 15–20 min. at 180 degrees Celsius.
> Mix 2 cups coconut with 1/4 cup sugar.
> Spread lots of raspberry jam over base.
> Cover with coconut mix and bake 5–10 min. more.

Oh, yes! Footprint Pie indeed.

AMERICA THE BEAUTIFUL

Sitting at lunch one day, having supped my soup I observed in front of me a gaggle of three elderly ladies enjoying camaraderie and conversation. Loudly. As their luncheon came to an end, the sprightliest of the trio reached deep into a shopping bag and pulled out a brightly colored jacket, shook it with a flourish, and held it against her bosom for the approval of her friends. It was a stunner in anyone's language. Both arms were boldly striped, one with red and white, one with blue and white. The rest of the gaggle laughingly encouraged her into a little parade. Jacket on and arms akimbo, she twirled for her joyful audience. The back of the jacket was red, white, and blue—and emblazoned with enormous, shiny stars.

Then, out of the corner of my eye I saw one of the darlings lean in close to a friend and heard her whisper, "She may want to change the buttons. They look a bit American, you know."

I hid a smile.

VEHICULARLY CHALLENGED

VEHICULARLY CHALLENGED?

They really said that. Many things challenge the brain, the body, and the emotions when you move into a new culture. Some things make you smile.

I was traveling along the freeway in sunny California on my way to Santa Barbara. For the past forty-five minutes the traffic had been dawdling along at approximately two miles per hour. Inside my trusty Merc I had occupied the tedium by speaking with colleagues on the telephone, listening to music, and dictating letters until I finally decided I would listen for news of the road situation and traffic flow. "You are vehicularly challenged," the announcer said. Was it a joke?

GIRAFFE MAGIC

I had to return to San Diego's world-famous zoo before I departed California. I had powerfully precious memories of a day there with Toby when he was fifteen years old. So I went. With Casey. We walked all day.

Nearing sunset, and the giraffes were still on our list. We stood as still as mice. They were so beautiful that I was mesmerized. I had forgotten how tall. I had forgotten how majestic. Father giraffe was pacing. Mothers, sisters, aunts, and cousins were discussing life's issues. Huddled. But one teenager watched me. Or I thought he did. I called to him. I had not called a teenage giraffe before. He came to me. He stood facing me directly. Huge eyes looked deep into mine, eyelashes proud against the setting sun. We spoke.

I do not remember what I said, nor do I remember what he said. I was transfixed. I reached my arm out and over the hedge into the space between us. Huge eyes continued to hold me. Long neck stretched towards me. We stood, strangely connected. Then, across the space, slowly and gently as a child, he stretched out his long, blue-black tongue to lick my hand. "No one will believe this," I whispered to myself. A giraffe kissed me. I may never wash this giraffe lick off my hand. Casey and I smiled our disbelief.

A week later I was back in Australia. I called Rachael in Mossy Point, but she was in Sydney. So her sister and I had a delightful and somewhat lengthy conversation. I had never met Rachael's sister, but I told her the story of being kissed by a giraffe.

"I have a giraffe story too," she said. "When my children were little, we went to the Melbourne Zoo. A giraffe did not kiss my husband, but it drooled on his jacket. The jacket was suede. I took the jacket to the dry cleaner the next day. "There is a stain on it," I said, pointing.

"What is it?" they asked.

"You are not going to believe it," I said.

THEN AND NOW

Exactly thirty-six days since 9/11, it was Wednesday, October 17, 2001. I was fifty-eight years old. I was single. I was a woman. And I was off. My beloved Mercedes E420 was nine years old and had 100,394 miles on it. Kell, of Calibre Motors, told me that it was a strong car and should do just fine on the trip. Trip? I felt like Lawrence of Arabia beating across the desert on a camel. I needed loud music and lots of applause for this epic journey, a drum roll, at least.

But as they say, everything else was then, and this is now. I planned to drive from Orange, California, as far as Indian Wells—just past Palm Springs—to stay with Lennis and see the new home she and Harvey had built there. "Jillian," she admonished gently, "make sure you do not load the inside of your car. You don't want to look as though you are a traveling girl." Great advice. And such was my intention, but despite my best efforts I did look exactly like a traveling girl.

"It may be time you came home, Mum," said Luke, my elder son. In the six years I had been working in California he had never said that. But it was now the October after the September 11 that changed the face and psyche of North America forever. "I am worried about you over there." He had never said that before either.

STANDING UP IN SALINAS

Shivers of cold breeze blew the fur of my coat up into inverted commas around my face, which reflected my bemusement back to the camera. I was standing alone in Salinas, Kansas, at the refuelling stop for the multitudes of small aircraft flying from one coast of the US to the other. I asked the pilot to take my photograph in front of the plane. There was small chance that I would ever repeat this adventure as the only passenger in a chartered jet flying from Orange County to New York City.

I was urgently needed in New York, and because my CEO preferred to travel by private chartered aircraft in order to avoid airport crowds and to be able to meet non-stop with his staff, no time was to be wasted. On the road with him meant eighteen-hour days. New York meetings done, we could fly back to base in Orange County. Hence, a chartered jet was summoned, and I was on my way.

"You will not believe what I am doing!" my face says. It also says, "I do not believe what I am doing." Willis would have laughed. I laughed too, tossing back my head.

Traveling as the lone passenger in a private jet, I was in my own cocoon of thoughts, enveloped in a world above the earth between home in California and work in New York City. I was fortunate in many ways. I had been offered opportunities I had not dreamed of, and here in Salinas, head back and laughing, I was being offered opportunity.

HEILKO

These days of my life were held together with what feels like fine silken thread—spider thread and what Heilko called *a constant series of small adjustments*. I was listening and feeling for the smallest of adjustments with all my being. I have to tell you about Heilko. He was the only person I knew personally who had a passion for tightrope walking, sometimes known as funambulism. He was so committed to this that he erected for himself a triangular tight rope right above his backyard. On this he practiced daily. I begged him to demonstrate, and he did, wearing special soft shoes and holding a long wooden pole. He was a star. At seventy years of age, he was remarkable. Later, as we celebrated his cleverness I asked him to explain the key to such balance. This was his reply: "It is not any one thing; it is a constant series of small adjustments." I was struck by the brilliance of that and thought of it often as I wended my way through the endless learning life offered me.

A GIRL HAS TO LOOK GOOD—OR, CLOTHES IN A PAPER BAG

Since a girl has to be prepared for any contingency, and since my immediate contingencies did not include working for a living, I sent six wardrobe-sized boxes of clothes, four square boxes of clothes, and one suitcase full of clothes to Florida at the cost of $502. All the clothes I sent were for play. I was sitting on the lawn in a glorious Sydney park not long after my unplanned and unexpected divorce, feeling daunted. Next to me was an alarmingly ordinary-looking gentleman who shocked me into a spasm of thinking and exploration, which has not yet ceased. "Go for bliss, Jillian," he said as he got up to leave. I would. Wearing a different outfit every day.

In preparation for my next new life, despite the fact that major amounts of clothing had been shipped, my car was still laden. I was bringing six boxes of files containing the myriad details of my life. I dared not let them out of my sight. Without their contents I would have to leave this planet. I also had one large suitcase, which I could hardly lift, containing clothes for the trip. One hatbox, with a seriously gorgeous hat inside it, was with me because the hat was so wonderfully outrageous that I had to have it near me. Various practical accoutrements filled all the small gaps.

BE VALIANT

Close to sunset I pulled off 60-E to check my map. Traffic had been very slow. For one knee-weakening moment I felt unsure that I was heading in the right direction, which was daunting. My Argentinian friend Nicholas had admonished me to, "Be valiant!" as I left California. I would do my utmost. My map reassured me that 60-E was correct. I could see an Acapulco Restaurant and a Chilli's and Center Point, but only God and the locals knew which suburb I was in. I was glad they knew. It was reassuring in a wondrously useless kind of way.

Triumph—as I completed the first leg of my journey. I arrived at the Vintage Club in Indian Wells, where Kristian welcomed me at the gate. Kristian, whose name sounds so Norwegian, was in fact from England. He had been there six years and said in his well-modulated accent so foreign to these parts, "The desert at night, with no other lights, is absolutely beautiful." He escorted me through the luscious grounds, which bloomed luxuriantly in the desert, to Lennis's and Hardey's house. Built into the side of a rocky desert mountain and over an artificial lake, it was only just this side of magic. Hollywood-gorgeous slabs of glass set into the living-room floor gave dramatic visual access to the lake beneath. The curved side windows tuned your eyes to the harsh desert mountains. A gigantic slab of unpolished travertine reached across the living room, carrying with it a narrow linear flame ten metres long. This slice of drama was the fireplace. Three dining room tables waited, triumphant, to seat family and friends. Twenty-four external fountains gushed their waters to a pool with a swim-up bar fitted to seat twelve. Showers were available inside or outside the house. A gymnasium to rival any at the Ritz Carlton awaited guests. An aquarium filled with brightly coloured exotic tropical fish overarched the entry into the home theatre, where leather reclining seats were as good as any that first-class airline travel provided.

At 1:10 p.m. Thursday, October 18, I followed Lennis in her white Porsche down the hill, having spent the morning grasping and gasping at what it meant to have the biggest and best home in the desert. It had the feel of Richard Meier's Getty Center in Los Angeles. I would drive to Tucson, Arizona to stay with Thomas and Anne Miree, which would be about five-and-a-half hours of adventure. The Vintage Club was a very beautiful place to have stayed in on my first night.

It was 4.55 p.m. when I made a pit stop at Love's in La Paz County, Arizona, forty miles east of Phoenix. Everybody and his uncle seemed to be there for gas or Marlboros. A sign said, GLACIER ICE COMPANY—PARTY ICE SOLD HERE. The newspaper was the *Arizona Republic*. On the wall was written, BUD WELCOMES RACE FANS, and BASKIN-ROBBINS—31 ICE CREAMS AND YOGURTS.

Under the astonishing Arizona sky at 6:00 p.m., the sun set behind the mountains. I drove through Phoenix with light moving quickly towards darkness. Sensuous strands of cloud resembling extruded fairy floss were draped across the sky and over the mountains, all brilliantly underlit with orange and coral and pink. The mountains were low and rough, the terrain desert, with stumpy trees. Air went deeply into my lungs under the Arizona sky. A Buddhist proverb says that if you are facing in the right direction, all you need to do is keep on walking. Facing in the right direction, I needed only to keep on walking, toward the east, toward Florida, toward Griff.

PARIS IN A PAPER BAG

I met Griff through my work in California. He remembered my sparkly jacket. I remembered his charm, energy, and good looks, which rivalled those of Cary Grant. He was effortlessly a Hollywood man, although in fact hailing from the Deep South. Griff told me that I was far too independent and needed to learn a thing or two from the southern "magnolias" he knew. "You do not need to get in and fix things yourself," he admonished. "You draw a little breath, lower your eyes, and say, 'Show me.'" But too much Australian "give it a go" attitude was in my blood, and trying simpering ways made me feel like a fraud. I did love to watch it though.

Griff was an addicted giver. From the moment we met he poured his deliberate, thoughtful, generous love all over me. He sent flowers to my office, where their beauty caused a few questioning eyebrows to be raised and a few tentative requests for the identity of my benefactor. I would drop my eyes and smile. Imaginations all around me moved into action.

He loved to buy me clothes, always choosing glamor with style utterly to my taste. "You are not wearing that! No," he would expostulate if anything I looked at was too practical. In preparation for one formal occasion, he sent a box containing an outfit which would have suited Princess Diana. If I spoke of a perfume I liked, he would order twelve.

Over dinner one evening he proffered a jewelry box, demanding that I open it then and there. "I have never seen you stuck for words before," he laughed at me as I sat speechless at the beauty of the necklace he had had made for me by friends of his who had opened a new business in Palm Desert.

Once, when driving in Florida he asked whether I had ever tasted Krispy Kreme donuts. I had not. Posthaste, we drove to the nearest store, where he parked the car with a flourish and dashed for the door. As he walked back to the car his grin was almost as big as the box he carried. He had bought a dozen. We ate them all.

Paris was his first overseas trip. Giddy with joy, he absorbed every delight that city offered. We ate and drank Parisian magic for days. Each morning he raced off into the fray, returning to smile me awake with fresh coffee and croissants. Paris in a paper bag.

DESERT FAMILY

I arrived at the Zwiers's residence. We met at Rick's Café, perched happily at the end of their street, for a little celebration over dinner. I ate half of Anne Miree's leftover dinner, drank a split of champagne, slurped a bite of mango sorbet, and drove to their home. Anne Miree was tired. Thomas was tired. I was tired too. It was corporate tiredness. They had redone the tiles in their kitchen. Thomas had been sent a book on the history of his Dutch family in the Netherlands, the Salamons, who immigrated first to Australia and then to the US. We perused the book and then dragged ourselves off to bed by 10:15 p.m. A six-hour drive and all the excitement, and I was poignantly aware that this was the last round with family for the foreseeable future.

The American flag my executive assistant Joanne had so lovingly given me before I left California had flapped noisily all the many miles by the right rear window of my car and had lost all of one side. Joanne had packed a treasure trove of practical goodies for my journey, showing her love right to the last minute of our time together. I would miss her.

The Arizona sunshine poured in. I slept well. Linda and Ernie called me from Australia at about midnight, loving me along the way. They had no idea what the time was in Arizona. They did not check. I did not tell them. I read a portion of a rather self-indulgent book Anne Miree left for me, entitled *Under the Rose: A Confession*. I needed to wire money to New York to Lehman Brothers. This was the first investment for me outside of real estate. God bless the money. It was the wisest thing I could think to do with it.

What could I expect with Anne Miree? It was always a funny day with her. By the time I got up and shampooed, had breakfast, unpacked and sorted a little, we were ready to head off for the thrift shops. Apart from drinking champagne and eating guacamole, this was our favorite thing to do in Tucson when we were together. The thrift shops provided me with a western shirt for an event that we were to attend that night. I also bought a pair of very good shoes for fifteen dollars; a beautifully elegant, French-looking coat in brilliant pink, brilliant yellow, and black with a little black dress to go underneath for one-hundred dollars; a beautiful patent leather bag for eight dollars; and a wonderful belt of heavy gold chain and cowhide for thirty dollars. That is all.

We celebrated over lunch at Loews Ventana Canyon resort, split a roast beef sandwich with onions and mushrooms, drank a glass of Sauvignon Blanc, and headed home a little weary.

STETSONS AT SUNSET

I washed and ironed the western shirt and decided not wear it. I decided instead on the sexiest spangly top I owned with skin-tight, black, St. John jeans, purchased at Nordstrom and duly shortened. Wearing Willis's Akubra hat, I presented myself as ready to go to the big western hoedown night. Anne Miree presented herself bedecked with a spangled western scarf, a flowing western dress, black silver-tipped boots, a black Akubra hat (the gift of a former boyfriend in Australia), and a beautiful black with silver bag. Thomas was similarly bedecked in brand new jeans purchased at a thrift shop for three dollars, wonderful thrift shop cowboy boots bought for twelve dollars, a beautiful cowboy belt tooled with his name at the back (also from the thrift shop), and a black Stetson.

We took many photographs of ourselves in front of the dramatic cacti with the sun setting behind the mountains.

Photographs were of Anne Miree with Thomas, Jillian with Thomas, Jillian with Anne Miree, Thomas and Anne Miree at the front door, Thomas and Anne Miree close up, and Thomas and Anne Miree from a distance. We looked wonderful.

Thus bedecked, off we went to Calgary Chapel in the Cadillac. Calgary Chapel is ensconced in a strip mall shopping center, which is divided into two sections—one being Osco Drugs and the other, Calgary Chapel. The people arriving as we pulled into the parking lot were not similarly bedecked. There were jeans and plaid shirts, and more jeans and plaid shirts, but not a spangle to be seen—and certainly not dramatic Stetsons such as ours.

We decided to arrive, nevertheless, and in we went. What a bad night it was. It was all so boring that we cringed at the thought of wasting our beautifully bedecked selves on the assembled throng. We ate our food and left as quickly as we could, sneaking out of the side door past members of the choir and into the Cadillac. And then, as luck would have it, the Cadillac would not start. Much trying, much discussion, all to no avail. Dead she was, very dead; "dead as a doornail," we would say. Having left the assembled throng without so much as a "by your leave," we were now forced to re-enter to beg for help. But even the gracious lending of their jumper leads did not set us on our merry way. Roadside service was called. A young man arrived looking seriously helpful. He checked fuses and other important innards of the car and did in fact get the car started, but he left us with the warning that it all may be too good to last. And it was. Off we headed as fast as we could. Thomas dropped Anne Miree and me at Rick's Café and drove on home, where he stopped the car. And of course, it would not start again.

Meantime, blissfully and determinedly unaware, Anne Miree and I ordered champagne, listened to the jazz band, and supped on fruit and cheese. Thomas returned, this time in Anne Miree's Mercedes SL. We talked about Afghanistan, the state of the world, Israel, WW II, living in Australia as compared to living in the United States, the pension, and what we would all live on in the next ten years. All having been discussed and nothing having been decided, we came home— Anne Miree shoveled into the back of the SL and Thomas and I in the front. With great difficulty we extricated Anne Miree from the back seat—cowboy boots, Akubra hat, beautiful dress, and spangled scarf all somewhat askew. We planned to drive to Tombstone on the morrow.

TOMBSTONE TREASURES

The morning of October 20 was spent with Thomas making arrangements for a new battery to be installed in the Cadillac. Much testing and trying the night before and much testing and trying early the next morning had brought no new life to the car. A tow truck had come. The driver had said, "It's definitely a battery."

Off we went to Tombstone, Anne Miree in the back seat and Thomas and I in the front. Tombstone? We loved it! We had a wonderful time. I was wearing Willis's Akubra again. I could see it was going to be a major part of this trip. I planned to wear it all the way across the United States. Looked good. Felt good. A very Australian look—a hat made from the fur of thirty-eight rabbits, they told me. Poor little bunnies.

Tombstone streets were swarming with people dressed in Western attire. Some of them looked absolutely gorgeous. There were people dressed in Western garb who looked as though they drank serious amounts of alcohol for a living. There were people who, for their living, re-enacted scenes from the 1820s, 30s, and 40s in this silver-mining town. There was a stunning pair of Harley-Davidsons, black and gleaming, smirking at us by the side of the road.

We wandered in and out of stores, looking for memories. The store I enjoyed most sported a dramatic back wall covered in an alarming assortment of spurs. A gentleman was leaning across the counter in the process of removing a spur from the boot of his customer. Sometimes it was difficult to differentiate between reality and illusion in Tombstone.

I found a store containing silver and turquoise jewellery. I was not much impressed with their offerings, so asked the proprietor if she had anything more dramatic. "I do," she said. Went to the back she did and came out with a beauty. I bought it. I love it. Made from a huge chunk of old turquoise, soft aqua and caramel colored, it was set in dramatic heavy silver. She said, "$250." I tried to talk her down. She would not come down. "Six hundred fifty dollars at an estate sale," she said accusingly. I knew she was right, and she knew I knew. I asked if she had any more that were similar in weight. "That is the *only* one," she admonished. Emphasizing *only*. Anne Miree was jealous. She kept saying she would have bought it if she had seen it first.

The next time I visited Tombstone I wore it out of respect and was surprised to be approached by four different old timers who asked me where I got it because that particular soft-colored turquoise was no longer mined in Tombstone. They were thrilled to see me wearing it, which left me even more thrilled to own it.

TREVOR AGAIN

I was single again after twenty-seven years of marriage and with family in Tucson, Arizona, when I was compelled to call Trevor, the brethren lad of the piecrust coffee table. Australian friends had called to tell me that his bride had died of motor neuron disease. A friend of mine had died from the same disease some years before, and I had watched the devastation of his body and that of his family. I could not bear the thought of the loss of all that innocent beauty.

Trevor and I had not seen each other or been in contact for more than forty years. He had returned from some years in the US to live in Australia. I was living in the US.

Because I knew he would not remember me, I had a little explanatory speech prepared. I would be another person offering sympathy at such a time. "This is Jillian," I began, ready with my little speech.

"Jillian!" I heard. And I thought I perceived an axis shift—slight but unmissable.

I was in Tucson on the first leg of a long journey driving myself across the US after six years working in southern California. He was on the first leg of a long journey too, a journey of a different kind. "You have given me something to think about," he said as we said goodbye. "Can I have your number so that we can keep in touch?" What had I given him to think about?

We kept in touch as I traveled through Santa Fe, Beaumont, Dallas, Oklahoma City, Natchez, on and over the bridge into Louisiana, and on to Destin—where I was planning to start another new life.

Christmas came, and with it the offer of a trip back to Australia from my boys. "My boys have invited me back to Australia, and I will be in Melbourne for a few days," I told him. "Maybe we can catch up over coffee."

"How will you get in from the airport?" he asked.

"I will rent a car," I said, all independence and efficiency.

"I could pick you up," he said.

"Whatever is easy," I said, nonchalant.

HAROLD AND RICARDO

I took up the hem at the bottom of my beautiful long, black, silk robe. Good thinking-time for me, sitting up in bed sewing. I was shot back in my mind to early July, when I was also sitting up in bed but for totally other reasons. My diary for that day reads:

Saturday morning 5:55 a.m.

Sitting up in bed I am.

I slept only two hours last night.

I was fired yesterday. By Harold.

Personally.

Leslie was there. Eyes frozen, moments of hate.

Rick was there too, hiding behind his moustache.

One awful hour it took. I have never been fired. Up until now, that is.

"Not fired," Harold had said, "let go. There is nobody I respect and admire more than you."

Right!

Driving down the freeway later, I called Ricardo, the charmer who had rushed into my life three months before—all blue eyes and careless money, and full of stories to keep you smiling for days. Surprised he was, but busy. "I will call you back in three hours, Babe," he offered. I was driving the trusty Merc, with Timotheous and Amanda Jan, down the Pacific Coast Highway toward Laguna when he called back. He had thought about me a thousand times last week.

"You did? Tell me what you thought."

"I got myself into a bit of a mess."

"You did? Will you tell me what kind of mess?"

"I got married."

"You did what?"

"I got married—to the girl I have been dating for the past twelve years."

"Oh my gosh!" as Casey would say.

He who told me he had no one in his life.

He who told me four days before that he wanted to come to Australia with me at Christmastime.

I had trusted him.

I had trusted Harold too.

"I want you to work with me for the rest of my life," Harold had said.

"I love you. You are the most amazing woman I have ever met," Ricardo had said.

This could well be the most astonishing day of my life. Fired and dumped all in one day. Let go and let down. I left my country. I left my boys. I left my home. I left my job. I left my friends. I left the warp and weft of life in Sydney with the flagrant light of the harbor and I took myself across the Pacific Ocean to California to work in a position that would consume me—mind, body and soul—for six years. It was my work. I loved it. But Harold had lied. And despite all the opportunities I had been offered, he had only wanted me to work with him for a part of his life, not for the rest of his life. Ricardo had lied too. He only wanted me for a part of his life, the part when he was visiting California. Practiced in the age-old art of manipulation, their advantage outstripped me at every turn.

After all that, I was taking myself into one more new life. Still a woman and still single, I was navigating both the roads of life and the roads of the American countryside. "Be valiant,"

Nicholas had admonished me. I would do my darndest, not wandering aimlessly anymore. I was determined to stride now.

AT THE GAS STATION

Fired I was.
O help.
Think money.
Don't think money.
Spend.
Resist spending.
Be frugal.
Relax.

Fired I was.
The future no longer luminous.
The future unknown.
Full of courage
I labored.
Full of fear.
Fear,
To be avoided at all costs.

Fired I was.
How could I have guessed?
Who would provide succor?
A safe place?

And then
There they were,
Floating and scudding
Towards me.
Fresh and crisp and green.
And mine.
Not attached
To anyone
That I could see.
Succor
For me.
Encouragement
For me.
Two bills.
Two five-dollar bills,
Floating and scudding.
To encourage
Me.

Inside
And in line
Ahead of me,
A plump blonde
Searched the pockets
Of her work apron.
Anxious.
Outside,
She searched.

Anxious.
I followed.
Anxious
Not to give way
To the desire
To give way to
My own need.
Have you lost something? I asked.
Ten dollars, she said.
I found it, I said.
O thank you! She said.

It was not mine.
I will have other saviors.

ANOTHER DAY. ANOTHER DOLLAR

I was a very fortunate but very tired girl. It had been a big six years one way or another.

Sunday, October 21. We met the family for brunch at Rick's Café. We each had two eggs, french fries, one slice of orange, and toast or a muffin—Rick's standard Sunday family breakfast duly offered at $3.95 per person. Once home, Anne Miree and I rushed straight to bed for a sleep while Thomas rushed off for a business meeting at church. At five thirty Jayson and Hilde came over with the children and their dog in tow and a fresh pizza in hand.

Rick called at lunchtime today to enquire after my welfare.

That was a major surprise. Very sweet of him it was, and very interesting, especially since he had been present at my firing, hiding well back behind his moustache. As I reflected that he was hiding behind his moustache on that occasion, I was startled to remember that his daughter, an extremely smart and capable young lady, had been fired summarily too, some years before. "Jealousy," he had told me. She had been managing far too many projects far too well for far too long. A clue for me as I orbited in the unexpected realm of the unemployed.

MURDER IN THE DESERT

One more night in the desert and I was emboldened to keep the external door to my bedroom open, allowing the desert breeze to calm me. The achingly brilliant canopy of stars viewed in this desert sky strengthened my soul as I worked to quell my raging fear of rattlesnakes, willing myself to believe that not even one will slither into my room.

A few months before, Thomas had decapitated one of these magnificent creatures right outside in his yard. He knew they were protected but considered that his seven grandchildren were protected too. His morbid fascination with these terrifying snakes became so great that he insisted that he show me the rattle that he had removed from the tail of the one he had decapitated with his shovel. Even separated from its body, the small, strange, skeletal arrangement of interlocking rings rattled death as he held it menacingly far too close to my face and shook it.

Their dog Leisel had come across the first one coiled beneath a metal ladder enjoying peace and tranquillity, arrogantly sunning itself in the Arizona sun. She barked her warning with enough fervor to alert Thomas, who belted it with such force that it had been uncoiled and mute ever since. Magnificent as it was, it had been carrying the portent of death.

After the horror of that rattle held far too close to my face, the next time I visited I was unnerved enough to feel certain that I could hear one shaking its booty in the night. Never before had I heard a live one, but the sound of that grotesque rattle had never slipped away from my mind. The papery dry rattle calling death was particular and chilling.

When I asked if it was possible that I had heard one in the night, Thomas told me that my imagination was up to no good. But he found it the day after that, sleeping a rattlesnake sleep and dreaming rattlesnake dreams in the sun right outside the front door—on the step where any of us could have stepped on it.

Because rattlesnakes roam in pairs, the one I had heard and he had found was possibly calling for its mate. He killed that one too. It was a grievous thing to do, but we had too many babes to watch out for.

PRIESTS AND THEIR WOMEN

I was mesmerized by my continued reading of the saga of *Under the Rose: A Confession* by Flavia Alaya, a gut-wrenching and dramatic story of a young woman who fell crazily into a passionate love affair with the priest and antiwar activist Henry Browne. Their affair continued throughout a tempestuous twenty years and the birth of their three children. All that time it remained absolutely secret. Until she wrote this book, that is. She waited until he died. She refers to Henry as her husband.

He retained his high-profile majesty, sense of power, and protection by the church—while she was left to birth and raise the children in anguished silence, essentially as a single mother, believing in his love but offered no protection. When Henry was finally given an ultimatum by Ms. Alaya, he left his parish and moved to be with her. But when the secrecy and intrigue left, so did the passion and the romance.

SURPRISES

Life is full of surprises—but with my little dramas of the last few months, followed quickly by the big dramas of September 11 in New York City—I was a little overdone with surprises. Powerful white men have been known to discard their women without a backward look.

"I've thought of you a hundred times," said Ricardo.

"It's not enough, I need a thousand times," I joked.

"A thousand times then."

He sent me bouquets of flowers so bounteous that I took photos of them.

"You are the most stunning woman I ever met," he said.

"Meet me in New York. Meet me in Paris."

"I want to come to Australia with you at Christmastime." He sat on my couch one Friday in July and said that. He was married the next Thursday. But not to me.

He bought me gifts. Clothes. Scarves. Jewelry. Sunglasses. Meals. Banquets.

"Why is it that when I eat with you, it is the best meal I ever had?" he asked.

"It's the company," I said.

He was generous. But he stole a part of my soul.

He talked of God. But he was dancing with the devil.

"I promise," he said.

He did not keep his promises. It was not that he got married. It was that he did not tell me. It was time for another story. It was time for my next new life.

MY NEXT NEW LIFE

Another night in the desert and my door was open, letting in the leisurely breeze. I was over my fear of rattlesnakes but feeling frustrated. My cholesterol was too high, which put me on a waiting list of eighteen months for Blue Cross health coverage. I was considered high risk. Thomas could have helped, being an expert on alternative medicine. Weirdly labeled packages arrived daily and were consumed with small bites of toast and sardines, or kippers. These death-defying morsels caused him to have a trail of Flipper-like malodorous cloud following him.

An email from second son Toby told me he had almost enough money saved up for his travels. He would be the traveling man in the family, while I was the traveling woman. Where would he choose to travel with the world in such turmoil?

AAA AND TRIPTIK

Anne Miree encouraged me to join AAA Travel Insurance. Their calm, practical help made me feel safer. I had planned my route, and they would prepare what they call TripTick-individualized maps for each leg of my trip from Arizona to Florida. On Thursday morning I was to set sail for New Mexico, about a nine-hour drive. I had originally planned to drive no more than six hours each day in order to protect myself from overtiredness. But as there appeared to be nowhere decent for me to stay in between, Santa Fe it was, for two nights.

Thursday and Friday nights in Santa Fe, Saturday and Sunday nights in Oklahoma City. Then down to Dallas Monday night, and onward and forward to Houston by Tuesday.

Anne Miree and I lunched at Versace, a beautiful Italian restaurant. Too much champagne and guacamole consumed, but they made up for me feeling a little slapped around by life.

FIXIT

I drove to a local car company recommended by Anne Miree to have the wheels of my trusty Merc balanced. There had been a shudder in my steering wheel that bothered me when I hit seventy-five miles per hour on the road. I sat myself down in the waiting area of Mr. Fixit and was happily reading all the latest and greatest in a mushy gossip magazine when a gentleman with startling blue eyes came out to me and said far too quietly, "Come with me, I have something to show you." Both his words and demeanor made me a little nervous. I followed him through the workshop to where my car was up on a hoist, looking as though it was about to give birth. Mr. Fixit, all low-key and deadly serious, pointed without a word to a huge bulge on the inside of one of my tires. It was what they call *separating*. Looking at that bulge, *I* felt like separating. "Could have blown at any time," he said quietly. The implications were alarming to say the least. I had not seen the bulge because of its location on the inner side of the tire and had felt only a slight tremor because of the strength of the Merc. "A smaller car would have thrown you all over the road," he said. "You would have known something was wrong."

Mr. Fixit recommended two new tires. I wanted four. I did not dare drive out of Arizona with anything less. I thanked God that He put it in my head to have the wheels balanced. They had needed a lot more than balancing.

NO AVOCADO

Four brand new Bridgestone tires later, I offered my thanks to Mr. Fixit and set off, but not before I had treated myself to the most wonderful bagel I have ever eaten. Einstein's Bagel House was an innocuous establishment amidst a group of other innocuous establishments. It was located midway down a strip mall close to Mr. Fixit, who was busily saving my life by replacing bulging tires with bulge-free tires. I demolished a bagel with chicken, sprouts, lettuce, tomato, and peppers—but no avocado. I had asked for avocado. I had asked for avocado three times. I had pointed to avocado and had said in the Queen's English that I wanted avocado. But somehow, I never did get any. But I did have good coffee.

It was fortuitous that I listened to that last tape on my little traveling dictation machine because I had said, "Good coffee," and then there was deathly silence. I had told many tales into the tape recorder, but that tape had reached the end of its little life, and I had not noticed. So blithely I spoke on and on, but nothing was recorded. It was an interesting thought, that all those words could be recorded somewhere. I read once of a person who believed that eventually we would be able to recover the voices from the past—out of walls and out of school desks and lecture halls. The idea of it fairly boggles the mind. All of the things that have been said have to be somewhere. Now that is a very scary thought. There are a few things that I have said in my lifetime that I would much prefer to be lost forever. As a child, I had an image of angels up there in heaven with quills, dipping them into golden ink pots and writing without pause into very large books. It may be possible that everything is recorded, but not necessarily by angels with quills, although that image is much more appealing than the use of digital equipment. "C'est mysterieux!" as my French friend Monsieur Polio would say.

After the bagel adventure I paid for the four new Bridgestone tires and drove to Dillard's department store, drawn by a mysterious force known only to women like me, to a counter where costume jewelry was selling at $2.99 a pop. Clearance! Most was marked down from forty-five dollars, with some marked down from fifty-five dollars. Being one for a deal, I purchased a few pieces. I reminded myself of a friend whose husband said of her that she was a great bargain shopper, the best he knew—in fact, she simply bought too many bargains. Upstairs, I bought Godiva coffee, the reason I went to Dillard's in the first place. Four packages of hazelnut—two for Anne Miree, two for Griff. Casey introduced me to that.

TRIPTIK

After the new tires, the bagel, the jewelry, and the coffee—I went to AAA to pick up the TripTick maps that had been prepared exclusively for me, marked in detail all the way from Tucson, Arizona—to Destin, Florida. "Your AAA TripTik, an exclusive Triple-A service, is the backbone of your travel package," they read. "The detailed, informative strip maps meet the needs of motorists traveling today's highways." Tucson, Lordsburg, Albuquerque, El Paso, Walsenburg, Amarillo, Oklahoma City, Fort Worth, Dallas, Houston, Lake Charles, Baton Rouge, Lake Charles, Jackson, Vicksburg, Slidell, Mobile, New Orleans, Crestview, Panama City, Pensacola. Enough.

Just the thought of driving nine hours on Thursday made me want to stay in bed forever. William, a precious friend from my years in real estate in Australia, called while Anne Miree and I were driving later on. Anne Miree made him laugh a lot. I decided I would call him back when we could have a more leisurely conversation. He had something on his mind. "He likes you," said Anne Miree. We had known each other for eight years, and he was a good man. He told me once that the kind of man I need does not exist. How could he be so bold? I should have asked him what kind of man he thought I needed.

Hilde prepared a dinner of mixed beef and vegetables with rice. It was a lot of work for a young mum with two little ones. In between young Isabella being sweet and having tantrums and being jealous and crying and laughing—the baby was having a little nip, as Hilde said, or a little sip, teething all over his coaster and being his sweet little self. We sat and talked while burgundy candles dripped all over the tablecloth. Jayson and Hilde puzzled as to why their aunt would want to drive across the United States, alone.

Thursday, October 25, and I headed out for Santa Fe, New Mexico, a nine-hour drive. As I journeyed into a state I had not ventured into before, I was filled with a great sense of freedom. My trip. My car. My thoughts. My music. My books. My friends to welcome me along the way, and my precious friend Griff to welcome me at the other end.

MY LITTLE RED SCOOTER

When I was in primary school, each morning Willis would drive me in his trusty FJ Holden and drop me off at the school gate before he headed for work at the barracks on St. Kilda

Road. He would park the car, walk around to the trunk, and lift out my beloved red scooter. This was a relatively heavy contraption, which I am sure would have been secondhand. Post WW II almost everything we had was secondhand. But I loved it. It offered me the sense that I could go anywhere and explore anything. Each day after school I would zoom it down hills, walk it across parks, or carry it across a swollen creek—testing new ways to travel home. It was my time. It was my space. It was freedom. Now, in my trusty Merc and on my new journey, I felt that freedom again. There was no wind in my hair, but I felt it nevertheless. Singing, "On the Road Again," I was back on my little red scooter.

GRIFF

I read *Under the Rose* until midnight and finished it, then slept very well until about 6:30 a.m. I was in tears when I said goodbye to the family. Griff called to tell me that all my boxes of clothes had arrived in Destin. He had had cupboards custom-made for me, and would hang my clothes. An amazing man, he even welcomed Anne Miree and Thomas to come to Florida for Thanksgiving, and of all things, to bring the dog.

For six years Griff had offered me encouragement, support, refuge, fun, laughter, friendship, and unquestioning loyalty. He had held me up from afar in my Californian life. His generosity and his spirit were life-giving. I will be forever grateful for this precious, warm-hearted man who encouraged me in a hundred ways. Now he was offering me his home for as long as I needed it, as I watched and waited in my next new life. It was a joke that I should not look as though I was a traveling woman. The car was not quite loaded to the gills, but it was very close to gill level, gasping for air enough to speed me on my way.

I started off with 100,991 miles on the clock. I spoke with Maureen in Santa Fe. Rosalie had offered me this relationship. I grabbed the offer as they say, with both hands. I loved my friends and had many—but did not know anyone in Santa Fe.

On Highway 10 headed east, the vista in front of me was filled with the low, ruggedly turreted mountains of Arizona. A sign said, BENSON AHEAD. I drove sixty-seven miles slowly, wending my way out of Tucson while speaking with Casey, who was still grieving the death of her husband. I called Rosalie to tell her that I was wearing the St. John knit jacket with leopard print given to me the last time I was with her. I felt her love for me as I wore it. It was armor for my journey.

A DINOSAUR BY MY SIDE

On the seat to my right, ensconced in a Godiva chocolate bag, was a tiny cloth dinosaur, as ugly as you can imagine. Perhaps it was a frill-necked lizard? It was given to me by Anne Miree as I left her. The lizard or dinosaur was shrouded in white bridal net. What a weird and wonderful combination. No one I knew except Anne Miree would offer this gift. She knew I would understand. It was a, "Don't you cry!" present. It reminded me of one of Willis's sayings when things were tough: "Backs to the wall."

Trusty Merc turned me towards Tombstone, EXIT 303-3 MILES. I was on Highway 10-E headed towards stunning mountains—and totally, utterly and completely in God's hands to care for me along the way. Huge billboards punctured the countryside. FUN COUNTRY RVs, they said—and then, MARINE INCORPORATED, WENDY'S—EXIT 303-1/2 MILE—KIDS MEAL $1.99, NEW DAYS INN-OCOTILLO—EXIT 304. And finally, RED'S CAFÉ—EXIT 303.

Huge angel wings, closed like wrought-iron gates with light seeping through the feathers came into my mind again and again. They were opening up in front of me. It was mysterious, as my French friend would say.

My little veiled bride sat pertly beside me while the whole surrounding area looked as though dinosaurs had roamed. I passed Exit 318 and a sign that told me, DRAGOON ROAD-1 MILE. From a distance, it looked to me like Dragon Road. Huge rocks lay in untidy heaps along the side of the road, spewed out by an enormous eruption. Boulder upon boulder grasped the desert land in front of me. Rugged mountains thrust skywards. This was grand territory. It was such a reminder of the outback of Australia. The road hewn between these rocks had grass here and there, and lumpy clumps of earnest, bright-yellow bush. I drove up a slight incline and the Merc did wonderful things for me. Willis would have loved it.

FJ HOLDEN

When he first purchased his new six-cylinder FJ Holden, Willis could not wait to take the family out for a showing-off. As we approached a small hill on Elgar Road, he said repeatedly, "Watch this! Watch this!" Not knowing what I should be watching, I glanced all around our new mechanical wonder. Finally, as we reached the top of a small bump of a hill, he said, "See that! We didn't even have to change gears!" He was triumphant. He never lost his joy in owning that car, cutting and polishing it to within an inch of its life. One of the children who lived next door to 45B came with us on one of these adventures up the Elgar Road hill and then down the other side. As we hurtled down at all of thirty miles per hour, she gasped and blurted out, "I feel gizzy!" I have never hurtled down a hill in my car without smiling at the memory of those words.

VENTURING ON

This freeway was buzzing. Where were all these people going? I thought it was *my* adventure, but on that road at that time it looked as though half the world was on an adventure. I stopped at the top of Texas Canyon for a little refreshment, and there the restroom said, WOMEN ONLY. NO PETS. Didn't somebody there think that is a little incongruous? I should have thought to take photographs of all the signs that amused me.

Back on the road at 10:50 a.m., and immediately in front

of me was an SUV pulling a wagon covered in a tarpaulin that was frantically flapping in the breeze. The driver seemed oblivious, but I had a horrible feeling that the whole thing would take off, blinding me. I got away from it before I was enshrouded like my little dinosaur companion.

At 11:22 a.m. I was still on Highway 10-E. I crossed Richards Lane, and immediately past it on the left was a sign saying, PECANS, WALNUTS AND WINE. I was in the midst of gastronomic delight myself, listening to a five-CD set discussing life and food in Provence, France. Gastronomic delight for me was also a homemade peanut butter and prickly pear jelly sandwich, my sustenance for the journey. Anne Miree had made it for me, a final offering of love, as I left the family.

Before I left, I took from the refrigerator a small piece of leftover steak, which had been maintained in some semblance of health and freshness since the disastrous Western night hoedown event we experienced on the first night I arrived in Tucson. The dog, delighted by the odor, sat begging at my side. But it was all mine. Sorry darling, drooling, begging baby, I needed this protein for my journey.

With 136 miles done, three times that and I would be in Santa Fe. I passed a sign that said, DEMING—PURE WATER AND FAST DUCKS. I wondered what in the world that was all about. I would pass through Deming on my way to Santa Fe. I could hardly wait to see the fast ducks.

At precisely 11:42 a.m. I passed over the border into New Mexico. WELCOME TO NEW MEXICO—THE LAND OF ENCHANTMENT, a sign said. The mountains were slightly more rounded in this part of the high desert. There were no strident clumps of cacti, only small bushes and rounded fertile-looking mountains nestling. The sky was rampant blue; strips of cerise clouds stretched across it to the horizon. Flotillas of trucks paraded along the road, and from time to time a freight train and electricity poles moved silently across the high desert.

LOVE'S

I took a pit stop at Love's, somewhere west of Deming. I did not quite know where I was when I stopped. It did not tell me. Love's, with their iconic red heart in place of an apostrophe, is a family-owned North American chain of more than four hundred and seventy truck stops and convenience stores in forty-one states of the US. The company is headquartered in Oklahoma City. I came to love Love's. Irony! I could have been a traveling Australian advertisement for this most American of businesses. They offered everything a traveling girl could need: fuel, showers, and food from a variety of restaurant chains.

At Exit 22 there was Love's and Texaco. That was all. There was not a dwelling to be seen except for the low, flat building that I suspected was a Holiday Inn. Once again to the restroom, only to find another darkly determined notice on the door: WOMEN. NO MERCHANDISE PAST THIS POINT.

I followed a truck onto the freeway. Off to the right was a small dwelling that looked similar to the original Richards dwelling in Australia where James Dennis, the first of our

Australian clan, put down roots and lived with his family in the early 1800s. That was a bluestone shed, which looked a bit like a henhouse. I saw it myself when I visited the family farm in Mernda, outside of Melbourne. This building was about a tenth of the size of the henhouse-sized Australian one, and looked like a large and weary dog kennel. The door was gone, although the corrugated iron roof remained. The stone walls were daubed with an ochre coloring. Who or what could have ever dwelt in such a thing?

The James Dennis bluestone building in Mernda became the focus for a gathering of the Richards clan when Willis and Uncle Eddie decided it was time for a shindig before all the oldies dropped off the vine. More than two hundred came from all over Australia to celebrate. Willis told me later that, apart from his not remembering there was only one toilet on the Mernda property, the rellies all came bearing old black and white and sepia photographs. "The trouble was," he grinned, "very few could remember who was in the photos!"

I looked at him, with his balding head and double chin, and—galvanized by the thought of his imminent death—squawked, "Get out that old shoebox of photos now!" We sat together for hours while he remembered and I wrote on the back of each photo. Those old photos now hold a doubly precious memory—of the rellies and of a few moments captured for the two of us—like a frozen moment in my mind.

JILLIAN RICHARDS

A WEE DRAP O' THE DOIN'S

Isabella Murchie Capuano was my maternal grandmother, even though she was not my grandmother at all according to my mother, who hated her with a vengeance. She married my grandfather Francis Capuano when, as a newly immigrated gem from Scotland, she was about forty years old. By the time I was born she had been turned into a step-grandmother. How Isabella Murchie and Francis Capuano came to meet I do not know, although my best guess is that it was in a church-affiliated moment of lust for one or other of them, church being the basis of their society. My maternal grandmother had died, possibly from exhaustion, and my mother Annie Merle Capuano was left bereft at the age of seven. Annie Merle was the youngest of the nine children of Francis and Annie Merle senior, or at least of the nine that I have been able to track down. The next sibling in age to my mother was Adele, known to us all as Dellie. Fourteen years older than my mother, she was already married by the time her mother died. So, there was my grandfather Francis, a widower with a young female bairn to take care of. Maybe there was no lust involved after all. Maybe he was a wily old fox who simply needed someone able and willing to do for him and to care for his grieving daughter.

 Whatever the true story is, I will never know, as they all have now passed on to the happy hunting ground in the sky—and their stories have passed into the ether with them to be once again a part of the stars from whence they came, not to be spoken of by my family, even in hushed tones.

There was Merle, and there was Francis, and there was Isabella, and there was me. I, who knew nothing of the family intrigue, grew up loving Isabella. She showed her practical nature by crocheting collars and cuffs in white cotton, as was the fashion of the day. These she sold to a local store and used the income to stretch the meager pension she lived on. Her resilience, her thriftiness, and her uncomplaining nature captured me.

Isabella fed us a meal filled with wonder on the odd Sunday we visited her home in Elsternwick after church. Single fronted, her cottage had a long corridor down one side with rooms switching off to the right all the way down. The memory of her salt cod with white sauce and mashed potatoes is still enough to make my mouth water, although for some strange reason I have never cooked it myself. Perhaps I thought it would not be so good as Isabella's. Tapioca plum pudding with custard and cream was for dessert. I loved every mouthful. I was sure I could taste the love.

Francis Capuano died before I was born, and the only evidence I have of him is a photograph of a very handsome, dark-haired Italian man in profile. I have no stories except for the one where his father sailed to NSW, Australia, from the Greek island of Corfu with his brother, who was captain of the ship. He then jumped ship and walked to the Ballarat goldfields, and eventually on to participate in the Eureka Stockade. But of Francis I have no other anecdotes and no memorabilia. I guess that their family was not filled with joy as my mother moved through her teenage years and through the rest of her life with memories of her deceased mother buried deep in her heart. "They took me in to see my mother after she had died," she once told me. "I did not want to go. When I saw her, I knew that I was alone in the world, and I have been alone ever since." She was not alone, but the feeling remained. It was the only self-revelation I ever heard from her. She seemed to have shut off emotionally at the age of seven, and there she stayed for the rest of her days, not truly participating in a full life. She had a stepmother she hated and a father she once told me was "a very angry man."

Into this milieu I was born. Over the ensuing postwar years we settled into Christmas and Easter holiday routines, with the Richards family gathering one weekend and the Capuanos, another. At the Capuano gathering, Isabella Murchie Capuano's Scottish tapioca plum pudding—with pre-boiled threepences and sixpences poked in here and there—became to me like the vision of sugarplums dancing away in my head. Lashings of custard and cream were the norm, and there was the most decadent trifle to finish—and little mouth-watering gems of Scottish shortbread.

When Isabella died, I was living in the United States and was sorry I was unable to comfort her. "Please keep some of her treasures for me," I begged from afar. Her Elsternwick house was not much endowed with grandeur, but the old furniture lovingly shipped from her home in Glasgow, Scotland, so many years before held a sense of solidarity and solace for my soul.

I was grateful that I was named in Isabella's will and left

a set of silver soupspoons that were carried from one abode to another as I have traversed the globe. Their next journey was from Melbourne, Australia, to Gothenburg, Sweden, to be offered to my son Toby John. The loving memories remained as I travelled to Sweden with Isabella's offering of silver to pass on with a tale or two.

Isabella has to have been a lady of courage. Why did a Scottish lass aged forty years, leave Glasgow to travel to Australia? And then what induced her, a single lady of conservative taste, to marry an Italian widower with an unhappy seven-year-old daughter to raise? One of the many things that marked Isabella was the Scottish burr brought to Australia along with her strict Scottish upbringing. The burr is the sound of the trilling of the R with the top of the tongue. This burr surrounded many of us in Australia in the post-WW II years. Another marker was the fact that Isabella Murchie was a teetotaler. But as Christmas approached each year, and it became time for her to prepare the ingredients for her famous sago plum pudding, Isabella could not restrain herself and had to add a violent portion of what she called *a wee drap o' the doin's*. Now I wonder where these *doin's* came from. Did she venture into a grog shop? And if she did, what deep feelings of guilt ventured in with her? Or did she perhaps ask the neighbor who had come to her one day with an enticement of truly neighborly proportions? Would she respectfully consider whether he could use all of her long, narrow Elsternwick backyard to grow vegetables? He would be forever grateful, and keep her yard with pride. He was an Italian gentleman, and she had had an Italian husband. In return for this gracious favor, she could have all the fruit and vegetables she could manage to eat. Would she? She was a Scot, after all. Perhaps this intrepid neighbor, himself an immigrant from Italy, was the source of the doin's. I do wish I had asked more questions.

CUT GLASS AND SILVER

"No mum, they are not our style," Toby said.

But I found myself persisting with, "Are you sure?"

He came back with, "We do not really have anywhere to put them, mum. I don't think so."

I was offering my son gifts I considered to be of value, and now I felt somewhat bereft. I had wanted him to be grateful, pleased, and smiling with gratitude. Instead, I was left with a chest full of emotions for which I was totally unprepared. When I approached Luke later about the matter, he was even more definite. "I don't think so, mum. They are not our style."

It felt like a personal rejection. I was amazed at myself. I even wanted to cry. These were remnants of my paternal grandparents' lives that hooked me back to a strongly emotional sense of family. I wanted my children to be hooked too.

They had been wedding gifts to my grandparents Edward Duer and Ada Elizabeth when they married on my grandmother's twenty-first birthday in the year 1900. My father gave them to me not long before he died. I knew he had treasured them.

When I was a child, I had often walked into the enormous

pantry of my grandparents' home following Auntie Gwen, who reverently brought down the ruby-glass and silver biscuit barrel to use at the family gathering. "Here, you hold it," she would say. I felt like a priest at the altar. I could hardly breathe for the weight of responsibility. The silver lid and handle had been polished and the ruby glass cleaned until the whole thing seemed to me to gleam with a bestowed holiness.

My trip from the pantry to the dining room table filled me with pride and fear. "Humph," was all that Grandfather would say. He terrified me. But Auntie Gladys beamed at me, proud and encouraging. "Jill the Pill," she whispered and winked. The family quieted a little as they watched my magic journey. I trotted back to the pantry, where I was handed the pretty, feminine-looking cruet set. Fashioned beautifully of ruby glass and silver, it had so many component parts that it required a maid to keep it gleaming. Last of all came the heavily engraved silver teapot on its special stand with a burner underneath. I carried out this holy mission each year at the gatherings of clan Richards.

Together in my home for many years, these items brought back memories of good-natured banter; the smell of scones baking in the old-fashioned wood stove; and the look of Uncle Percy wearing his huge, heavily starched white apron, up to his ears in flour and clotted cream. And Auntie Gladys at the piano with her crazy dog on her lap, both singing.

I wanted my children to desire these items. They spelled out, "Don't forget me. Take me down and polish my memory from time to time when I am gone." There was much more invested in them than I had imagined when I offered them to Luke.

I got out the few photos of the Richards clan and looked at the images of my grandparents and reflected that I did not know them very well at all. They were old and unwell—and not much bothered with the young ones. But the rest of the clan filled the house with the good-natured laughter of country folk and offered their joy in each other's company along with the hot scones and clotted cream, and Auntie Gladys's homemade jam—transported with love all the way to Melbourne from Kyabram.

This is what I was trying to offer: family, fellowship, and food—the smell and sound of love and trust. But my boys were not there. They did not smell the scones or hear the cacophony of voices and the music and the dogs and the doors slamming. They had nothing of their own invested in my offerings.

So I swallowed my self-pity and decided not to give up. I worked the room a bit. Luke was to be in town for two days. The ruby-glass biscuit barrel, the ruby-glass cruet set and the silver teapot all came down out of my cupboard and were polished to their gleaming best, then displayed on the dining room table in the light of the setting Melbourne sun when he walked through my door.

"Oh, they are very beautiful, mum," he said.

"Are you sure you don't want them?" I asked, trying not to sound persistent.

"Well, maybe," he said, and by the time he left our home two days later he had said, "Let Toby decide what he wants. We will be happy with the other."

An email from me with photos attached, and Toby chose the teapot. "Because it is less likely to break in transit from Australia to Sweden," he said. "We will pick it up next time we come to Australia." I felt much less rejected, but I needed to tell more stories to make those early days of my life come alive for my boys. I was happy that these pieces would be where they should be—for the next generation to look at as they listened to fragments of their story. For a while at least, this precious part of our family story would be safe.

AUNTIE GLADYS

Everyone needs an Auntie Gladys. The second child and only surviving girl in the Richards quiver, otherwise full to the brim with boys, she set hearts alight wherever she stepped. Generous of heart and full of joyfully irreverent laughter, she sets my heart alight as I think of her. She filled life with a smile. Her gifts far outlived her life on this mortal coil.

She taught her dog to sing. She grew the sweetest tomatoes and bottled them. She became a scout leader in her beloved town of Kyabram. Her scones won every blue ribbon the country shows had to offer, and the cream on them tasted like the sweet breath of a cow.

From my point of view just above knee level, the Richardses were always adult, always together, always in Grandma Richards's kitchen, always telling jokes, always telling stories of the farm, and always giggling—well pleased with their own sense of humor. Gathered together, they would giggle like a lot of schoolgirls—high pitched and infectious. I would giggle too, although not having much idea of the cause of the mirth. Gladys would grasp my arm in ecstasy.

MISSED

I moved onto a little road with the grand title of Highway 26 that should have linked up with Highway 25. I missed Highway 25 in Deming. I misread the little curly cues and turns and tiny little tight things on my TripTik map—so I turned around, back to Exit 82B–Highway 180, the Silver City. A few miles of travel on 180, and I was onto Highway 26, which was really not a highway at all. It was just a two-lane road going through a country town on the way to Hatch. From there I headed for Albuquerque. I was surrounded on all sides by flat flatness—so similar to parts of the outback of Australia.

A billboard to the left had a black background, a white border, and white writing: IN GOD WE TRUST, UNITED WE STAND, it proclaimed. Great loyalty to this country had come to the fore since the terrorist acts of September 11 in New York City. Only God knew where such adamant national loyalty would take us.

I passed Starlight Village, a resort RV Park in the middle of nowhere. Both the word *resort* and the word *park* required a more than mild stretch of the imagination. A couple more miles of driving on Highway 26, and I passed a man who looked to be at least sixty years of age jogging along the side of the road, headed in the same direction as me. There was little of civilization to be seen apart from a two-lane highway and an easement following great electricity lines. Where was he coming from and where was he going? I did not plan to stop and ask him as I flew by with my dinosaur at my side.

The multitude of semitrailers, which were fore and aft all the way from Tucson to Deming, thinned out to a reasoned few, most of which were coming towards me. The destination of many must have been El Paso. A railway line ran along the right-hand side of the road. I passed two chimney stacks on my left. No other part of the dwellings remained. Somebody must have lived a desolate life in this remote place. What stories those stones could have told. At 1:30 p.m. I was still on Highway 26. It was still desolate. I hurtled past two gentlemen with packs on their backs hitching a ride. I would have loved the company, and I am sure they would have loved the ride, but "Not today, darlings."

OPEN MIND—OPEN HEART

I turned the radio off. In this wide-open landscape, I wanted my mind to be open and receptive. Hatch, New Mexico, was one small town. I passed a sign that said, AMERICAN STILL STANDS and another that said, CHILLI FOR SALE, then HATCH CHILLI EXPRESS, FRANCISCAN RV—THE FUN STARTS HERE, and finally, DO NOT PASS. There were dozens and dozens of chilli-stands lining the sides of the road. Thousands of chillies were spread out in the sun to dry, flattened out like red lizards on the ground. Thousands more were hanging in strands, all pulsing with color and fire. Then I was through it, just like that. That was Hatch. It was a vibrant surprise, and then it was gone.

The Rio Grande was a different kind of surprise. I had images of the Rio Grande as being enormous, overwhelming, rushing, brave and strong. But here it was, a slow, little, shallow river. I drove over it and I headed over to 25—25 North to Albuquerque. Suddenly, as I turned onto 25, to my left it was shockingly verdant. There were low mountains in the distance as I headed north into new worlds.

ELEPHANT BUTTE

On Highway 25 North there was hardly another vehicle on the road to disturb my pleasure. On my left was Exit 83 to Elephant Butte Lake, which sounded wonderful. It made me smile. Elephant Butte Lake sounded as though an elephant wandered in and put his butt down there with intention. When he left for greener pastures, the rains came down and the floods rose up—and the water came on down and filled that big old hole. Elephant Butte Lake. I liked it. Sun warmed my bones, streaming in through the window. Truth or Consequences was the name of the next town. Another smile for me. A brightly colored jelly bean.

Coming over a ridge in front of me were bare, bald mountains straining to hold themselves out of the flatness of the desert. There must have been hardy folk living in scattered little blotches of RVs and houses on the outskirts of Las Palmas. CAMPING, it said. Not for this girl, darling. It was wilderness.

TRUTH OR CONSEQUENCES

I passed two more signs made for a traveling woman to get her bearings. First, AUTO MUSEUM, and then TRUTH OR CONSEQUENCES. I had a strong need to know what stories were lurking.

I pulled off Highway 25 into Williamsburg, a tiny little town, to get gas. A beautiful young blonde, brown eyed and pony tailed, smiled at me when I asked her whether Truth or Consequences was really the name of the town. "Yes, it is," she said.

"How did it come by that name?" I probed.

"I really don't know," she said. And then she thought for a minute. "I believe it was named after a radio show years ago. The town used to be called Hot Springs."

"And now it's called Truth or Consequences?"

"Yes," she said. Her ears were pierced with a variety of studs from the top all the way down to the lobe on each side. Maybe ten, maybe fifteen studs per side. Amusing herself in Truth or Consequences she was, working at the gas station as well. A sweet girl.

I discovered later that Ralph Edwards, the host of the radio show *Truth or Consequences*, had announced that he would air the program on its tenth anniversary from the first town that named itself after the show. Hot Springs officially changed its name on March 31, 1950, and the program was broadcast from there. I would love to know which boldly courageous town resident opted for that name change.

AND I REMEMBER OTHER GIFTS

A Chicago lass she was, all liquid brown eyes and cunningly curved lashes in an oval face full of mischief. There was a grace in her. Her hair was braided tight as a piano string and her face was agleam with the joy of youth as she stood atremble with pleasure. Small puffs of cloudlike hope moved softly across her mind, then with the feather-touch of love, to her face. Her idea was love-filled.

I thought of this Chicago princess, as she stood atremble at the possibility of offering a testament of gratitude to her beloved teacher. Desire was strong in her, tightening her belly with anxiety, touching her emotions with hope. She wished to offer a gift which could show the measure of her love, but money was short in her family and her options were few. As Christmas came closer, she searched her home for a clue. There, all items of value were sorted and treasured. Rubber bands. Old paper bags. Pencil stubs. Bottle tops. Corks. String. And rags. Rags were useful to clean up spills or to wipe dust from the windowsill. It was agreed that she could choose a few of the best rags to take as a gift, a soft pile of love. She sorted, washed, dried and sorted again until her neat pile of rags was ready for careful consideration by the family. With their approval, she set off with a gift to rival that of the Magi.

Years after I first heard this story, I moved house once again, this time from Sydney, Australia, to Orange County, California. With all that I needed to leave behind and all that I needed to take, I wondered whether I should pack my own rags and transport them across the Pacific Ocean. Would I need them there? But more importantly, what would I do without them, my pieces of worn sheet that had been thoughtfully washed and torn into squares? Torn, not cut, as you must tear in order to have soft edges.

What would I do in Orange County if the outlet pipe at the back of the washing machine cracked and sudsy water made a run for the living room and I was caught without rags? An old rag in your hand can help you think straight, and with rags in hand I would definitely have that invincible feeling of "single girl in new country can handle anything."

Deciding that I did need the comfort of a few, and with a package of them in my luggage, I departed. Once in sunny and amazing colorfully entrepreneurial California, I was mildly surprised to discover that most people I met did not know what a rag was, nor what it was for. "Why?" they asked and looked at me the way Californians can. "If *we* do not need rags," they seemed to say, "then why would you? Australians sure are an unusual lot."

Apart from sunshine, machines ruled in California. Well, Hollywood ruled, but machines too. In that time of learning for me, the humble rag was a symbol of simple hard work, of love, and of comfort. Rags made sense; they always worked with me, never against me. In a complex and complicated world, I am normalized and gentled back into the powerful rhythms of the everyday as I work with a rag in my hand. And as I toil, the memory of that Chicago princess's profoundly loving gift lies softly on my mind.

TREES

I hugged a tree once, the way you do when all of life has caused so much desolation that the source of comfort and hope needs to be firmly rooted.

Trees have graced my life. At the very front of the garden in Willis's beloved home at 45B Bowen Street, there was an enormous eucalyptus. Over the years that I lived there, I was directed to look, to notice, to admire, to touch, to contemplate and to be grateful for that tree. Often. This magnificent gift presided over all Willis's comings and goings for more than forty years.

He had planted others: a blue spruce, a crab apple, a Japanese maple, and more. All were honored by his courteous care. The blue spruce was not just a spruce, it was a blue spruce. The crab apple produced abundant blossom and fruit. The Japanese maple offered brilliant color in autumn. I was exhorted, but never admonished, to love these and all his trees and to never forget what they offered. They became living anthems.

In California it was my joy to choose and plant trees of my own in the front yard of my new home. The back yard was already filled with the joy of citrus. I was living in the city of

Orange in Orange County after all. The previous owners had marked the birth of their daughter forty years before with the planting of an orange tree in the center of the backyard. By the time I was the owner of this tree, it had spread its wings and annually offered enough golden orbs to satisfy colleagues, friends, and neighbors. Even my little dog loved it, racing counterclockwise, frantic with the joy of her release on my return from work until she dropped from exhaustion.

The back fence was lined with dozens of varieties of citrus. Blood orange, lime, lemon, and more. The pair of blue jays that dominated my yard loved them. But the front yard suffered from the ruled-up look of an army barracks. Not a single tree adorned it. A concerted effort at softening and humanizing was required. Ruminating brought me a decision to plant three silver birches together in the middle of one patch of lawn. I needed their softening grace. It had become my great good fortune to meet a young man whose business it was to collect seeds from historic trees around the world and propagate them, offering his business as both a fundraiser and a lifegiver. I was enraptured by the thousands of his fledgling plants reaching for the sky. Each group of trees had a story—some seeds collected from trees hundreds of years old. He offered me the gift of a propagated tree or two, making thoughtful suggestions. A few weeks later I received two long tubes in the mail. One contained a slip for a southern magnolia propagated for Lady Bird Johnson from the magnolia on the lawn of the White House that had been planted by President Andrew Jackson in 1835 in memory of his wife, Rachael. There it had stood watch by the South Portico, its white flowers blooming through peace and war. For decades that magnolia was featured on the back of the twenty-dollar bill.

Prince Charles says that all he wants to do as he gets older is to plant trees. He has created an entire wood for his grandson Prince George.

I hugged a tree in a time of deep need, and it graced me with protection and comfort and love. Many have awed me. I have loved many. And I suspect they have loved me. I saw the ancient eucalyptus that graced 45B, and was so beloved of Willis, bend gently—offering shade as we took Willis to his final resting place. I hear them, the anthems trees have sung to me over the years.

BANANAS EES COMING

October 26. It was 8:32 a.m., and I was sitting up in bed in the El Dorado Hotel in Santa Fe, New Mexico, luxuriating in the thought of breakfast in bed. Twenty minutes later, "Bananas ees coming," said the beautiful Mexican lady who knocked at my door and brought breakfast into my room. Earlier I had called room service requesting Granola with strawberries and bananas, despite the fact that the room service menu said you could have only strawberries, or only bananas. "Oh, no bananas today," I was told, "we have no bananas today."

"Oh," I said, "I could have brought my own."

"I'm sorry," she said.

"That's all right," I said, "I'll have Granola with strawberries then." Twenty minutes later the knock at the door, and the beautiful senorita was there, arms full of love, along with my granola and strawberries. And bananas.

"The bananas ees coming!" she said, pointing to my bowl. We laughed together. Sisters.

WORDS TO LIVE BY

Sante Fe, looking out of the window at a blue sky perforated with streaks of cerise cloud, I reveled in the pretty trees—vastly different vegetation from that of southern California. Some had lost their leaves in readiness for winter; some were golden and glorious; and some were a bright, clean green—Elm, Desert Willow, and Mexican Elder. I could see a little faraway hill and little faraway houses, all bathed in translucent orange.

We had enjoyed a quite profound evening, Mary and I. She came towards me in greeting, pomegranate in hand. I love pomegranate. Vibrant childhood memories of opening a pomegranate and the wonder of it returned. So exotic. So many juice-ravished seeds. Such raw and vibrant color. I was transfixed the first time I saw one. "Don't open it in the car," Mary said.

"Oh, I won't. I want to carry this with me, this little part of the sunshine of Santa Fe."

Living in time yet living in eternity, one impinging on the other. This was part of the conversation last night. What a good time we had. What a brightly intelligent, tough lady she is. What stories she had. What a life. Close to death with

Epstein-Barr virus, she lost everything: her house—her job—her ability to walk, to feed herself, to dress herself—her confidence. She was at the point of suicide.

Later, I sat in a small courtyard under a magnificent tree and drank a glass of Riesling, looking at the hollyhocks. I wafted into childhood memories of Faith's house and her hollyhocks always looking staunch and satisfied. This courtyard was surrounded by adobe shops. The sun was shining. The trees were golden. It was very pretty in a Santa Fe kind of way. "Grapefruit salad?" I was asked. It came to me with many tiny green leaves and three small slivers of grapefruit. I think it was salad garnished with grapefruit, hardly grapefruit salad. I followed with white peach sorbet and berries, which were happy to speak for themselves,

Driving out of Santa Fe with the rising sun, it was 7:30 a.m. I was sated with memories of pomegranate and bananas as I headed for Oklahoma City. The road was all mine. High desert, trees changing color, rising sun, low hills—it was wonderful to be driving on a beautifully paved lane road with the sun rising and not another car to be seen. On the open road low hills settled around my shoulders.

OKLAHOMA CITY

The AAA TripTik told me it would take ten hours to Oklahoma City if I traveled at an average of fifty-five miles per hour. The gentleman in the garage at the El Dorado Hotel, who helped me by adjusting the air in my tires, said it would take ten to twelve hours. "Oh no!" I said, "It can't be twelve. I have to be in Oklahoma City for dinner at six." It will not be twelve hours. I will arrive in Oklahoma City at exactly the right time, I had decided.

MOVING ON

I adjusted my clock. I had my head in gear for daylight savings. Clocks went back an hour. In Australia they went forward an hour. I called Timotheous and Amanda Jane in Australia. Applications were in for their visas for permission to work in Colorado. Brilliant musician and friend Timotheous, as Minister of Music in a large church, and Amanda Jane in the occupation of her choice. They were involved in so many of the decisions that were exactly those I had to make when I left Australia. When and where to store all household paraphernalia? When to move out of the safety of home? To move into a serviced apartment? Not to move into a serviced apartment? To move in with family for a while? Not to move in with family for a while? To take a vacation? To resign? Wonderful choices at this moment of transition. It feels like the moment before a baby is born. Hold back or push?

Timotheous and Amanda Jane were staying with me in California the day I was fired and dumped. They were on their way to Colorado to discuss conditions of their possible appointment. We enjoyed each other over dinner, and I told them I had been called to a meeting with my boss, alone. This was unusual. So I said, half laughing, that I was either going to receive a raise in salary or I was going to be fired. We planned a lunch together the next day to farewell them. They waited while I went to my meeting and were sitting in my car in the parking lot when I came down wrapped in a halo of disbelief after the firing. They were heaven-sent angels for such a moment. Amanda Jane had had a similar experience a little earlier.

Did I still want to go to lunch?

Yes! Not only lunch, but champagne and lunch. Or perhaps just champagne.

Did I want Timotheous to drive?

No. I was fine. This, through cascading tears which were close to blinding me.

"I need to call Ricardo," I blubbered. "He would want to know."

I did call. He promised to call back soon.

He called back as promised.

He got married! He what?

So there we were, the three of us, careening down the freeway to Laguna, laughing and crying. All of us on a journey into the Never-Never.

SUNSHINE ON MY SHOULDERS

Incomprehensible forces were drawing me away from California to a new life in Florida, which I planned to love. We had talked about death—Mary, who very nearly died a couple of years ago, and I, who had nearly died last year.

I wandered the streets of the city square in Santa Fe, New

Mexico, fascinated with the art, the wonderful old etchings, and the beautiful old sepia photographs of proud American Indians. The one photograph that took my eye was about six-by-eight inches, of an Indian gentleman in full headgear. The photograph was taken in profile, head and shoulders only. I loved it on sight. That would be the one I would choose. A short time later, momentarily stunned by the twenty-five-thousand-dollar price tag, I decided I was not ready to spend twenty-five thousand dollars on a hauntingly fabulous frozen moment.

The streets were a contented haze of seclusion and secrecy. The whole town whispered and sighed, secrets buried as deep as a tomb. A row of American Indians sat with their backs against the wall the length of a whole block, stoic. Blankets were spread in front of them and covered gently with silver jewelry, carefully prepared for tourists. Nothing had the edge I could sense when I was transfixed by the profile of the proud gentleman whose portrait I did not purchase. Rounded bodies sat forward, protecting their craft. One woman with an exquisitely beautiful face entranced me far more than the offered adornments.

I went to the Cathedral of St. Francis, which contains the oldest Madonna in the United States. It was calming. The cathedral had been restored as a place of joy. People were sitting on the benches at the back, relaxing. I knelt for a while behind a row of Hispanic women, still and straight-backed, looking with awe at the Madonna. A side chapel had a sign warning me that it was FOR PRIVATE PRAYER ONLY. It was simply and sparsely furnished. An old gentleman garbed in sombre black was sitting in the second-to-the-last row, deep in private prayer. It felt it would be an interruption to go past him, so I sat behind him in the back row. Then I knelt and I felt the presence of God on my shoulders. I wanted to cry. "Sunshine on My Shoulders," sang John Denver in my ear. I had no doubt that this journey was for me.

FOUR HOURS LEFT

A retropharyngeal abscess that was misdiagnosed for three weeks had put me in peril the year before. I was readying for yet another working trip across the US when an earache began to bother me. With two days to go before I needed to board my flight out of California, I considered it expedient to visit my local GP. He looked carefully into my ears and confirmed, "'A bit of an infection. It is a little red in there." Antibiotics were ordered in the hope that the infection would calm down. I returned to the GP the next day, even more concerned. Not only was my sore ear not calming, it felt worse. More antibiotics were prescribed, this time the size of small horse pills. But, yes, I should be fine to fly.

By the time I reached Houston I was feeling as though I was in trouble, with the level of pain ramping up hour by hour. A good friend and longtime resident of Houston took one look at me and used her influence to get me an appointment with the pre-eminent Ear, Nose, and Throat specialist in town who tended to the likes of Pavarotti. Off I trotted the next morning.

It was their expectation that I have a hearing test prior to the consultation. I did not want a hearing test. As far as I knew, I did not need a hearing test. I wanted the infection treated and the pain reduced.

The ENT looked carefully into my ear and after some lip biting and lip pursing, sent me off for an x-ray. Off to the hospital I went in a cab, waited in a cold, dreary corridor, had the x-ray, and with that in hand took a cab back to the ENT specialist. One look at the x-ray and he stated that the radiologist had taken the wrong x-ray, and I should go back the next day for the correct one.

Meantime I had the need to cancel and rearrange appointments all the way across the country. And meantime I was beginning to feel seriously unwell, with the jabbing pain causing me to start from the shock of it. Second x-ray in hand, I returned to the ENT. He studied it and grimaced. "I need to call my colleague," he offered over his shoulder. Colleague arrived and the two stood, white-coated, in front of a screen to which my two x-rays were pinned. Much chin rubbing and quiet conversation ensued. They finally half turned to me and beckoned for me to stand in front of the backlit images of the inside of my head. "We have had a good look at these," he said. "The radiologist says there is an abscess, but we do not agree. No abscess—no abscess–no abscess!" This was accompanied by the loud clicking of his fingers in front of x-ray one, x-ray two, and finally—in front of my face. They had well and truly decided.

Back inside his examination room he peered once more

into the depths of my ear. "I think," he said loudly, "that you have a zoster."

"A what?"

"A zoster. Here, I will write it down for you." I still have that little yellow piece of paper. "I think I will just pierce through your ear canal while you are here to relieve the pain."

I am forever grateful for the shadow of horror that moved across the face of the attending nurse. When he produced the barbaric curved needle he intended to use, I moved away. I did not think so. Pavarotti or not, I did not think so. "Then we will put you in hospital for a day or two to see what is up." But by then I did not trust him, and I demurred.

So I was onto a plane again, armed with even bigger horse pills for pain and antibiotics the size of car tires. The journey to Florida was lost in a world of coping, endeavouring not to frighten my fellow travelers with the uncontrollable jumps that lammed me against my seat with each spasm of pain. Griff picked me up at the airport and did not like the look of me. I did not much like the look of me either. But duty called, and we attended a work function that evening. By the next morning my body just wanted to lie down and stay, so Griff bundled me into his car and off to his local GP. This gracious man listened to a shortened version of my story, examined me gently, confirmed the radiologist's point of view even without the x-rays, and sent us posthaste to the Pensacola hospital x-ray department for confirmation.

The look of disbelief on the Pensacola hospital radiologist's face when he looked at his x-rays was enough to warn me that I was in serious trouble. Within minutes I was wheelchair-bound and headed for admission. I did not even have a toothbrush with me, but neither was I too worried about that or much else, except that I could not concentrate on how I would deal with the appointments I had to keep.

By that evening I was being wheeled down the corridor of the hospital, flat on my back on a gurney, watching the huge ceiling lights popping past me one blink at a time. Griff was holding my hand—blessing me with his love, nurses were scurrying, and tears were rolling down my cheeks. I could no longer keep myself moving. I had given way at last. I needed someone to help me. I had been self-sufficient for so long, emotionally and physically. Now I could do nothing.

"I do not want to frighten you," said Griff at the door of the operating theater, "but this is very serious."

In the operating theater I was suddenly looking up into the face of an angel, the local ENT surgeon who had been called urgently to come to my aid. He grinned down at me. "We will look after you. What you have is a retropharyngeal abscess. We need to operate now. I will go in through the back of your throat. We cannot go in through the side of your neck, it is too dangerous." And then? Nothing.

Very bright lights and, again, that angelic face was close to mine, grinning. "If I didn't believe in God before, I would believe in Him now," he said. What was he talking about? "You would have had four hours to live." He nodded, serious now. "I was operating at the base of your brain, praying, "Mary, Mother of God, help me." He saved my life. That wonderful hospital and its wonderful staff saved my life. God intervened. It was not time for me to leave this mortal coil. Not just yet. Griff and the surgeon and the hospital staff had pulled me back.

Griff brought me silk sheets. "You are not sleeping in those," he scoffed, pointing at the perfectly clean and starched hospital sheets. The sheets he brought me were soft lilac, and healing came through them. He also brought me silk pyjamas, and a toothbrush and toothpaste, and flowers, and all the other loving treasures he could think of and his loving arms could carry. He called my Florida friends, some of whom drove across the state to visit me. One loving couple, ever thoughtful, brought a fragrant foot scrub and sat at the end of my bed chatting while gently massaging my feet. My sister flew in from Arizona.

Considered something of a miracle in that loving Catholic hospital, I was visited by dozens of doctors, most of whom had nothing to do with my case. They wanted to look at me. Flowers engulfed me with their love. A night nurse slept close, but I was too ill to ask her for help.

"If you did not believe in God before, you will believe in God now," the surgeon had said to me. He had encouraged my life force. Abundant love was also shown in the form of a room filled with fragrant blooms sent from across the country, and card after card told me it was time to look after myself.

I was mystified. I ate well, I exercised diligently and on a daily basis, I laughed as often as I could find humor, nails and hair were all in order. What did it mean? With much time to be still, I deliberated and cogitated and asked God to show me what was so obvious to others but not at all clear to me. Into my mind came these words, "You have learned how to perform, now it is time to learn how to live." Time indeed.

DRIVE FRIENDLY

On a CD playing in my car Aaron Neville sang me a prayer. On the side of the road two crows worried an early morning breakfast of carrion. I drove Highway 285 South, headed to Freeway 40, which would take me all the way to Oklahoma City. At five to eleven central time I crossed the state border from New Mexico into Texas. The sign said, WELCOME TO TEXAS. DRIVE FRIENDLY—THE TEXAN WAY. Drive friendly? What an interesting use of language. I was surrounded by flat, harsh country, listening to a book on tape.

I stopped for gas at Alanreed, Texas, 79002. A small, cream-brick building was covered in carelessly colorful cartoons. ROUTE 66—, it said, ALANREED AT LAST. A painting of grandma in her yellow Ford sat astride the wall next to a small cage-like attachment that purported to be Alanreed Jail. Across the front draped a huge sign, ROUTE 66. On the door, *Y'all— business is welcome, but please give us a hand by keeping only ten cowpokes at a time in the store. Yours sincerely, Deputy Dog.* The American flag was flying across the front—a painted banner, dramatized with eagles and Indian headdresses. More signs proclaimed such delights as clean showers, washers and dryers, beverages, groceries, ice, and gifts. A small notice in the window said RED MUD. Must be some kind of a Texan thing. Red Mud.

By 1:40 p.m. I had crossed the border into Oklahoma. It was greener. Ploughed-up greener. Big blue skies draped overhead reminded me of Australia. I loved being under the big blue sky.

Driving so far yesterday wore me out. Dinner with Mary had been really stimulating, and I observed with interest that, when I am with very intelligent and deeply thoughtful people, it draws out of me new and penetrating thoughts. This is not so much because of questions they ask; it simply happens in their presence.

I DO LOVE OKLAHOMA

Sunday, and I stood with sunshine on my shoulders, looking out of the window at Johannes's and Isabella's ranch in the eastern part of Oklahoma, a daringly beautiful seven thousand acres. Isabella drove three hours for us to get there. Built ten years ago, the ranch house, including the grand fireplaces, was constructed of local stone. Above the main fireplace was a mounted moose head—to the right an elk. I was in huntin'-shootin' country. From the back terrace I scanned low grass, beautiful trees, and a creek. A low hill rose behind the creek, melding with a stunning mixture of evergreens and deciduous. The deciduous were changing color, rustic and golden. Cool breezes gentled me. The sun warmed my right shoulder at 3:50 p.m. on the first day of daylight savings.

Ten hunters went out with Johannes after we had enjoyed an eastern Oklahoman special lunch at Cookson's Corner, with ribs to remember. I was so full after those I could hardly eat the catfish I ordered, which was light and fresh, even though in batter. I felt embarrassed to leave so much.

Sebastian was with us. A business friend of Johannes, he was a Columbian living in Miami. He traveled to Columbia every month for family business. He has an interesting story written all over his face, but he was not telling it. It was his first time hunting in eastern Oklahoma.

We drove to Ten Killer Lake where Johannes and Isabella have a boat moored at the marina. They go out sometimes at night, quietly, in the middle of the week. How beautiful. Isabella told me that she has had an easy life. I think she has in lots of ways. A former Miss Oklahoma—a beautiful, sweet, spirited person she is. A lady.

COCONUT CREAM REDNECK

Now they tell me that truth is stranger than fiction. Here I was sitting in the kitchen of the Schneider's house, and Davey was cooking his mother's coconut pie. "Mama—it's Mama's," he said, as they say down south.

"What did you say you are?"

"Yeah, I'm a Mississippi Redneck. This is Mom's coconut pie and I'm from Mississippi originally, but I live in Clarksdale on the Mississippi River now, and we are just sitting here whipping this pie up."

"I want the story of the pie," I begged.

"My grandmother originally made this pie, and then the

recipe was passed on to my mother, and then she gave it to me. It has always just been in their heads. Nothing has been written down before. I really struggled getting this recipe, because she really didn't know, she just had to guess at everything. So that's kind of the story on this. So, you can see it's thickening up real nice now."

"Would you tell the assembled throng what other things you are doing here while you are in eastern Oklahoma?" I asked.

"We are on a deer hunting expedition, but we haven't been successful yet. I haven't, so hopefully tomorrow maybe it will be a little different."

Now, I could tell this was one loquacious gentleman. Active in other ways too. Born for the stage, cooking coconut pie and hunting deer. He also said Tasmania was his favourite place in Australia.

"My buddy lives in Bronte's Heart, Tasmania, Australia. His name is Cliff, and occasionally I go down and spend time with him, and then he comes and spends time with me. So, the last time I went I spent a month, and this last year he spent six weeks with me. So, I don't know—next time I go I will have to stay longer than he did, so each time it's getting a little longer—we go each way, so…"

"How did you meet this man?"

"Oh, I was rolling around in Tasmania and I walked in the store, and he had a deer head mounted on the wall, and I asked him about his deer head, and he said, 'Yeah, I got that thing.' Tells me the story about it, and we got talking, and he said, 'I'm coming to America in the fall—going to Idaho on a hunting trip.' I said, 'Well come on down and visit with me,' and he said, 'I'll do that.' He called me up about a month later, and the rest is history."

A BOY CALLED SHIRLEY

I loved listening to this. Here I was in the middle of the US on my own special journey, and here he was telling me a startling little bit of his.

"Tell me about Mama. What was her name?"

"Her name was Charlie-May. She was the first born in the family. And then the next one was a boy, and his name was Shirley."

"Why?"

"I'm really not sure. They've never told me that story. They never shared that with me."

Talk about the tales of a wandering woman—I was having the best time. Sunday, October 28. I was sitting up in bed in my own bedroom in the hunting lodge. Dinner had been a right-royal movie in the making. Davey, the self-proclaimed redneck who lives on the Mississippi River had made two coconut pies to die for, which were presented to the assembled throng to enjoy as dessert. Out of his pocket he produced a piece of paper with the recipe written on it. The recipe had originated with his grandmother and was passed on to his mother as a precious part of her inheritance. Davey had carried it in his head for years. But for this particular hunting trip, "Just in case, I wrote it down," he said, waving the scrappy little piece triumphantly. It was the most amazing coconut cream pie I had ever eaten. Sweet as syrup, it slid down, smooth as silk.

Davey sent the recipe for Mama's Coconut Pie to me weeks later. This is exactly the way it was written.

MAMA'S COCONUT PIE

> 3 eggs (room temp) Separate yellows & save whites for meringue
> 3/4 cup sugar
> 4 heaping tLB of s-ring flour
> 1 3/4 cup of milk
> 1 tLB vanilla
> Combine Yellows, sugar, flour,
> milk and vanilla in sauce pan
> & cook on high stirring
> constantly & turn down heat
> as pudding starts to cook.
> After Mixture thickens, remove
> from heat & Add 1/2 stick butter
> & coconut (A cup to cup & half)
> Pour this into cooked (browned)
> pie shell. I add some grated
> coconut on shell before cooking.
> Beat egg whites on high & half
> way thru Add 3 tlBS of sugar & 1 tea
> of Vanilla. Beat until stiff.
> (over)

Spoon meringue on top of pudding.
Sprinkle some coconut on top and brown in 375Deg oven enjoy!

It was deer-culling season, and oversight was by members of the United States army. The men had been out hunting all afternoon, splendid in their camouflage gear with bright orange vests and hats for safety. I rested on the massage chair, read a little, talked a little, and listened to Isabella play the piano. We walked over to the shed for dinner. Just that, it was a big corrugated-iron shed. Inside, a rough wooden trestle table stretched down the middle, covering a large part of the concrete floor. Deer heads arrayed around the walls, stared balefully at the goings on, mute in the alien surroundings. Cement tubs at the end were for mighty amounts of food preparation and dish washing. All meals were considered lovingly and with great pride. Those appointed the year before the deer-culling season to take the honored position of cook had huddled for months in order to surprise us with their very best offerings. Hence, grandma's pie. Chicken, fries, coleslaw, beans, and bread were for dinner. Camp style. Army style. Huge men in camouflage gear with orange vests and hats sat down, ate heartily, told stories, and laughed.

To my right sat Sebastian, dark eyes full of stories. To my left. Lawrence—husband of Natalia, Isabella's older sister. Across from me sat Davey, who had produced his magic coconut pie. He's been to Tasmania twice—two times more than I had been to Tasmania. Now I had the name of his friend to call when I visit Tasmania. Don't know when that might be.

My latest redneck friend found it hard to believe that this Aussie girl had never fired a gun. Outside we all went for various gun cleaning and preparation exercises. I, doing my level best to look the part, was wearing Willis's Akubra. I needed the story of the gun. I was about to shoot something. "Is it a gun or a rifle?" I inquired. I was about to shoot whatever it was for the first time in my life, and this gentleman was going to tell me what it was that I was shooting.

"Okay. She is shooting a Tennessee squirrel rifle, which is a .50 calibre. It's not a flat lock; these guns were built either in flat R or percussion. This one happens to be percussion, round ball, 70 grains of 3F powder. And some of the terms on it are quite interesting. Have you have ever heard the term, 'Don't go off half cocked?'" I had. "Okay, the cock is the hammer. So if you half cock it, it won't fire. So that's where that term comes from. The term 'Flash in the pan?'"

"Yes."

"Comes from the pan on the flintlock when it goes off. It's real quick. It just flashes, and that's called flash in the pan. It's something that happens real quick. 'Lock, stock and barrel?' Here's the lock, the stock, and the barrel. It's all of it. There are several terms like that. The term 'cock' comes from a rooster. A cock-rooster, which is the hammer. It looks like a cock with his tail and his head and that's the hammer of the gun.

"I shot my gun this morning and I need to shoot it and

unload it so I can clean it—and I'm going to let her fire her first shot ... how's it going here .... So here she is."

I did shoot that rifle, fraught with so much history. I shot it at a one-gallon plastic bottle filled with water. Davey was a great teacher. The first time I missed. Just. The second time I hit the mark, and held the bottle up, triumphant, for the camera to record a little bit of Oklahoma-Australian history. That was enough shooting for me. The poor, sad carcasses of the deer that had been culled, hanging without glory in the shed, did not draw me to the hunt.

OKLAHOMA CITY

Tuesday morning, October 30, 2001. I was sitting in my car in the visitors' parking lot in front of the Oklahoma City Capitol. A huge crane hovered above. A dome was being added. Its skeleton scarred the sky. Large administrative buildings flanked the capitol on either side. A dome would soften the skyline. I called Carol. We enjoyed ourselves when she came to California for the first time in thirty years to celebrate her birthday. Carol worked in Governor Keating's office, and I would take the chance to say hello.

Casually dressed in a pale-blue tracksuit purchased at the Pelican Hill Golf Club in California, I was hardly appropriately dressed for the governor. I was dressed in preparation to hit the road that afternoon. A friend called from Houston to tell me she had heard on very good authority that it was possible that the next terrorist attack could be in Houston tomorrow!

Oh, Lordie. "Please do not tell anybody—do not let it get to the papers. My husband is furious with me for warning you, but I think you should be careful, and I think it would be wise not to come into Houston on the October 31st." It had been my plan to go in then. Such highs and lows. I called Casey. She was feeling a little depressed. She had been to a funeral and was beginning to feel the fear of terrorism.

I had dinner with Ian and his beautiful new girlfriend Andrea. He planned to propose to her at the White House when he would be a guest there in December. "We will get married in May," he said, "and she won't work. We'll make babies." God bless them. His friend was to call in during dinner to meet me. A billionaire. "A little rough," he said, "A little southern, but a good man." How rough could a billionaire be? He did not call in.

CAR WASH 1-2-3-4

Susan served at the gas station in Oklahoma City where I stopped. Susan, who had no teeth in front except for one dark little peg, was heavyset. She wore no makeup. "Car wash?" the pump had asked me politely. It was the first talking petrol pump I had seen despite having lived a total of sixteen years in this country. My car had been urging me towards a car wash for a while. I had traveled all the way from California having washed only myself. I filled the car with gas at the pump. "Car wash?" It asked. "Yes or No?" Yes. I pressed the Yes button. "Select type," it demanded, "Number 1—Winners Circle,

Number 2—Fast Track, Number 3, and Number 4." I pressed a button. Nothing happened. Zero response, except that the pump once maddeningly more asking me: "Car wash? Yes or No? Select type." Twice. Three times. Four times. I pressed diligently, round and round, but all I could ever rustle up were the same robotic questions.

Two young men were filling their car with gas right across from me. Bright blue eyes, fresh faces. "Can you help me?" I asked. "Have you ever had a car wash here?"

"No," they said, "but let's see if we can do it." They were very polite in that special Oklahoman way. The first one was no more help to me than I was to myself. Then came his other half—a brother, I think. Same blue eyes, same fresh face. He was no more help to me than I was to myself either.

So inside we went. "Oh, that keypad's not working," said Susan, "but it's cheaper inside anyway."

"Well that's good," I said. "How come it's cheaper?"

"Well," she said, "we've got two for one. Buy one, get one free."

"Oh, I'll have one of those too," said the blue-eyed, fresh-faced young man now standing next to me at the counter.

"It's all right," I said. "I don't need a second car wash. I won't be here. I'll give it to you."

"Oh, thank you," he said. "You do it for someone else later," I said. "You give someone else a free car wash, another day."

Sitting inside my car in the car wash, I remembered the first time I took a car into a car wash with Luke inside. He was very little, and I hadn't warned him. He was terrified—poor, beloved child. What a terrible thing for a mother to do. He might still need counselling to get over that.

I had woken at ten past eight, and only then because the telephone rang for Isabella. I had slept more than nine hours, dreaming weird dreams. I told Isabella the story of my Argentinian friend, Lucia, so excited to see an old boyfriend after forty years—four children of hers and goodness knows how many of his. She and her husband arranged to meet the old boyfriend at an airport in Germany. "I was so excited I was trembling," she said with her dramatic Argentinian flair, "but when he came towards me, he was an old man!"

ALWAYS ENUNCIATE

After breakfast I found my way to Zoe at the local beauty salon. Zoe was a toughly wonderful Oklahoman girl born in Texas. Married at seventeen. Married for seventeen years. Her husband, who was a house painter and very successful, started to play the horses. It ruined their marriage. After seventeen years it was over. Divorced for nine years, she had had a boyfriend for four. He was sixteen years younger. "I resented my husband," she said. "It wasn't jealousy, I just resented the fact that he wouldn't work, and he played the horses, and we lost everything. I couldn't live like that." She, too, had had her experiences with single men and was learning how to make her way in this new and unusual world of singleness after so many years married. "I don't like speaking lazy," she said, after a slip of the tongue. I smiled inwardly. "My mother said, 'I don't like you speaking like that. Enunciate.' So I said, 'Mother you don't like me doing what? What is *enunciate*?'"

I went up with Andrew in his prop plane for a one-hour spin over Oklahoma City. I loved every minute of it. He expressed surprise that I did not get sick and was not frightened.

I went to the Capitol and spent about an hour with Carol, who has worked for the Governor for years. I shook hands with the Governor and spoke with him for a few moments. I took a few photos and was astonished that there was no obvious security at the Capitol. I spoke to Ian about it. I spoke to Carol about it. I spoke to Isabella about it. "But we are not used to needing security in Oklahoma," they told me, "no one in Oklahoma would dare do anything." In these times? I am surprised.

RISK AND CHANCE IN LIFE

November 1. All morning I changed addresses and names on credit cards. I changed back to my maiden name, Jillian Richards—finally, after eight years. "The reason for the change of name?" they asked me. "Divorce or marriage?" Divorce. Eight years on and I was finally changing it. I would just be me, not me attached to anyone else.

I sent photographs to all and sundry. To Luke, Toby, and Melissa. One to Trevor of the piecrust coffee table too—wearing an Akubra, my arm around a deer hunter with his shirt pulled open. Inside, his T-shirt says *Australia*. On the back of the photograph I wrote, "In case you think I always wear a tiara."

I watched a television program, a documentary on sex change, particularly in the sixties and seventies, and the controversy which still lingered around it all. One riveting story was of a twin, born a male child. For whatever reason, and only God would know what that could be, his mother decided to have his sex changed to make him a female. Mother and doctor conspired. It happened. The child was named Raelene and raised Raelene. When Raelene discovered, at the age of thirteen, what had happened to him, he immediately changed back to being a boy. Life had been difficult for him. Married now, at the very end of the documentary with camera focused on the strange, drawn face of Raelene— now a man, now married—he said, "Eventually you end up being you, because you are human and because that is the way it is."

SORRY RAY

It was 11:00 p.m. on my last night in Oklahoma City. As we drove home in the car, Johannes and Isabella talked together about what they planned to do. "Oh," they said, "we are going to hear Ray Charles. Would you like to come?" Would I like to come? Of course, I would like to come. I absolutely love Ray Charles and have not heard him live. "Fifth row seats," they said. But I felt it was time to go. These two go out almost every night. They love each other. It was wonderful to watch.

Dallas was a three- or four-hour drive. I passed through

Norman, Oklahoma. I had been told of a wonderful museum in Norman, The Sam Noble Museum of Natural History. "Dinosaurs!" Dinosaurs discovered in Oklahoma. Dinosaurs from the West. American dinosaurs. I stopped there but first I went downtown to visit the Oklahoma City National Memorial.

TERROR IN OKLAHOMA

Constructed on the site of the Oklahoma City bombing, the Oklahoma City National Memorial honors the victims, survivors, and rescuers of the April 19, 1995 bombing of the Alfred P. Murrah Federal Building. Although the history of terrorism attacks in the US or against Americans is long, it was unknown to many. That is, until September 11, 2001, when planes flew death through the World Trade Center towers. I watched it on television as it happened. "War!" was my instant thought. It was.

On the news all day they kept saying that they were going to blow up bridges—the Golden Gate bridge and other bridges in California—at peak-hour time, November 2nd. Terror. Drama. I heard Tom Brokaw talking about the fact that embassies were blown up by the Afghanis, and that they put a boat into one of the American warships in the Persian Gulf. The American people seemed inured to such attacks until planes blasted through the World Trade Center. Deep terror did not seem to penetrate the psyche so long as it was happening in another country. It took this to wake them up.

LIMOUSINE RIVER

I was invited to a fundraising dinner in a barn. Money raised was for one hundred seventy hospitals across the United States, particularly for children in crisis from disease or accident. A reception was held in the ranch home: red brick, Georgian style, three years old, and huge. An aquarium in the games room completely covered one wall. Another wall had a television screen measuring twenty-by-twenty feet, divided into a multitude of sections. Bronzes. Wide hallways. Thirty-foot ceilings. Valet parking. Mahogany kitchen as big as a house. At this ranch they engage in sophisticated genetic work on Limousin cattle.

Reception over, we were all driven down to the barn in a rolling river of limousines. The barn was huge, with walls lined with hundreds—possibly thousands—of ribbons, banners, and rosettes as well as flags from various countries. Four hundred guests sat to dinner. Chairs covered in black taffeta. Tables covered in black taffeta and cowhide. Orange table decorations. Candles. Favors were tiny platinum Stetson hats and Stetson key rings saying *Stetsons at Sunset*. A Country and Western singer by the name of England performed with his two friends on violin and guitar. A former Miss America was there with her brand-new fiancé. Business, big Oklahoma business, was discussed openly.

My hostess told me that her husband gave her a baby zebra for her last birthday. The baby zebra, now seven months old, has been aptly named Spot.

Back home, we drank Grand Marnier.

Dallas, and then Houston. I would move out of Oklahoma and back into a wild world of terrorist threats.

IN GOD WE TRUST

I ordered ten copies of Ken Duncan's book today. Entitled *America Wide: In God We Trust*, it was produced after Ken's thirty-seven exhausting trips from Australia to the United States for the purpose of photographing in every state of the nation. It was an exhilarating adventure for Ken, culminating in release of the book in September 2001. Who could have planned that? These were appropriate gifts for those who loved me on my adventure.

Milt called today. He said, "God is showing you that He loves you." Elizabeth marked a map as I traveled across the country.

Friday morning, November 2nd. Johannes took me to his office to say hi to Macey, whose parents-in-law live, believe it or not, in Niceville. Johannes is such a gentleman that he opened the doors and came down to say goodbye at the car. The skies were gray clouded as I set off for the Oklahoma City National Memorial Center. Their brochure said, "This is the story of the largest terrorist attack on American soil. April 19, 1995 began like any other day. Here you will see highlights of routine morning activities and everyday life in Oklahoma City."

A rewrite of this brochure was in order. We had now lived through September 11, 2001.

I could hardly bear it. I found the Oklahoma City National Memorial Center emotionally exhausting. Closely surrounded by the story of the bombing of the federal building and the photographs of the 168 people who died was more than I could bear. And the little children. All the beautiful people. I stayed only one hour. It was too hard and too confronting.

I checked my phone as I emerged into the life-filled pulse of the avenue. One message. Anne Miree called from the Tucson Medical Center. She was taken into hospital yesterday. Her blood pressure was over two hundred. She had woken with her face drooping alarmingly on one side. "They do not yet know the cause. They are going to do MRIs." I cannot believe that I am emerging—from the celebration of bravery and courage in the face of death—to such news. I had hugged her goodbye only a few days ago.

SHOES FOR HORSES

I was given directions from a lady at the art gallery, which somehow caused me to totally miss Highway Interstate-35 South. As I didn't find it, I drove around a little, found a Bank of America, and took some cash out. Then I drove around a little more. I passed the Veterans Hospital, the Drug and Rehabilitation Center, various churches, and a gas station called Mercy USA. At my first Walton's Supermart, a gentleman checked my tires, checked my oil, and told me everything was fine, which made me feel much more secure. I wanted to tip him, but he said, "No, we are not allowed." What a shame. Out of Walton's, I headed for Robinson Street and then drove three or four miles to I-35.

I passed the Oklahoma Horse Shoeing School South Campus. Then, a sign said, SCENIC TURNOUT–1 MILE. Then, SCENIC TURNOUT–1/4 MILE. Off I swung from I-35 South on my way to Dallas, and once more I drove across the border from the state of Oklahoma into the state of Texas. DRIVE FRIENDLY—THE TEXAS WAY, the sign says.

HOUSTON

Monday dawned bright and sunny in Houston, Texas. I slept until 9:00 a.m. I went with Beryl to the St. Regis Hotel in Houston to meet friends for brunch. After that, we did girly things. We went to Marshalls and tried on clothes. We even fiddled around in a gold warehouse. I came home exhausted and dived for my room. After a little rest, I had to drag myself up and get ready to go out for dinner with a gentleman called Gordon. He turned out to be a lawyer—a sweet young man, once he got over his shyness. A recovering alcoholic, he had been a barrister, and had been able to do all of the analyzing of any case as though it was a chess game. All of the pieces moved around in his head, and he could put them into place easily and always win. When he went off the booze, he lost the ability to do that. Instantly. It never came back. "I've gained other things, though. I had to grow up," he said. "You can grow up if you want to."

David told me a story tonight as we sat in the back of Beryl's car, driven by Mark on the way to dinner at Tony's. "People are different here from those in New York," he said. "In New York, you know, when there's traffic they honk in an attempt to have the person in front move. It's not what we do here in Houston. One of my friends came in from New York," he said, "and he pulled up behind a huge truck. The lights changed and the truck didn't move. So my friend leaned on the horn. The truck still didn't move. So he leaned on the horn a little longer. The truck still didn't move. After the third attempt he looked up to see the door of the truck opening and a huge Texan stepping out wearing his Stetson. He walked slowly over to my friend's car, laid his arms along the window ledge, leaned in and said, 'Where are you from?' 'I'm from New York,' said my friend. 'I'm sorry, but this is really what we do in New York—we tend to honk the horn if somebody in front doesn't move.' 'Aha,' said the Texan, 'In New York you honk. In Texas we shoot!'"

I suspected David was pulling my leg.

For dessert I had ethereal zabaglione. I loved it. It was enough for four. I ate enough for two.

Pearl picked me up at noon. We went to the Brownstone Restaurant to meet the remarkable Janice for lunch. When she came in—a little late, a little breathless—she looked at me with shining brown eyes and said, "Jillian, you look superior." Then she looked at Pearl with shining brown eyes and she said, "You know how some people are buckles and they hold you together like a good belt—and some people are like brooches, they are like a wonderful decoration. Well you two are like buckles and brooches together. You both hold me together and decorate my life." At the end of lunch she said, "I feel fellowshipped."

We spoke of many things, time and space, and life and love. She said to me, "You will know by the flowers." She was being prophetic. I will watch for the flowers. She didn't talk about me having been in prison but she used a similar word, and she encouraged me to not have to be "doing." She said, "This time you will discover that you are loved—not because of what you do, but because of who you are."

GOING HOME

Luke called. He and Toby had put all their frequent flyer points together and made reservations for me to return to Australia, leaving December 11th from New Orleans, and returning to the US January 16th. Five weeks' vacation. Deliciously self-indulgent.

Pearl bought me an itsy-bitsy satin skirt and tiny sweater at the resale shop, La Perla, and it had been marked down from two hundred dollars to one hundred. She also bought me a spangly little sweater—purple and gold and white. What a generous person she is.

Pearl and Beryl and I had lunch with Holly. Beryl and Holly have known each other for twenty-two years. Holly is a beautiful, stately matron with deeply dyed red hair. Tall, she carried herself with the kind of confidence that comes with major success. A developer, she and Beryl met twenty-two years ago when Holly was presenting a talk on construction and Beryl was at the very beginning of her own career as a developer. They set up their own organization for women in the construction industry. "I was never building any more than sixty houses at one time," Holly said to me. She told us other stories of her life after I asked her how she got started as a developer. "I was hungry," she said, matter of fact. It explains everything to me. She carries a .38 given to her by her mother. Her grandmother always carried a gun; always had a gun in the house. Grandmother lived in a two-story, wooden-floored, frame house. One night she heard what she presumed to be an intruder downstairs and fired the gun straight down through the wooden floor. Another time a great flock of birds was squawking and squawking outside her window, annoying her with their squabbles—so she shot at them right through the glass windowpanes. "That," Holly said, "is life in East Texas." She and Beryl laughed. Both East Texan women. Last night Holly went with some of her friends to a Red Hussy party. Fires my imagination.

TRUTH IS BETTER THAN FICTION

The next startling story she told was of a lady I will call Betty. "I was working late one night." she said. "It was about nine thirty. I was in my office in the display home of the attractive homes I was selling, finishing up my paperwork when an extremely dirty and disheveled woman knocked at the door and asked to use my restroom. I said, "Of course you can use my restroom. You look as though you may need a coke or a cup of coffee too."

"Yes," she said, "I certainly would like that." They visited for a while and the unexpected visitor left.

The next morning a beer truck pulled up outside Holly's office. A fellow carried in two crates of beer. Holly said, "I believe you have the wrong address. I haven't ordered beer."

"Oh," he said, "this is a gift." Holly had no idea from whom. She made some enquiries, to discover that the family of the woman who had knocked on her door the night before owned a brewing company. One intrepid woman helped another other intrepid woman who was dirty and disheveled because she also owned utility companies and had been underground, checking services in an emergency.

There was a time when Holly needed loan money from a bank, and was working really hard to get it. She was in strife when Betty called her with an invitation for lunch. Holly said, "I'm sorry, I'm very busy," and explained what was happening.

Betty said, "All right."

About forty minutes later a woman from the title company called Holly and said, "I don't know what you are doing, but we just had somebody deliver dollars in cash to pay your loans."

A few minutes later, when the phone rang it was Betty. "Well that's done!" she said. "Now you'll have time for lunch with me."

It came to pass that Betty told Holly why she was so dirty and disheveled that first time they had met. Betty ran utilities companies for ten counties of East Texas. The one thing that people always wanted was to have their toilets working. If they weren't working, they would call and expect somebody to deal with them efficiently, to listen, and to get the toilets repaired quickly. A hands-on employer, she often went out with her men to oversee the repairs. So that night, dirty and grubby she was—because she had been down a manhole, checking on the things that had gone wrong when the toilets backed up.

Another time there was a problem with the telephone in the office of Betty's company. All the telephones were out, except for one line into her office. After two days of her trying to get assistance from the telephone company, a gentleman finally arrived. Betty said to him, "You are not leaving here until all the telephones are fixed."

He said, "Ma'am, you do not understand. I do not repair telephones. I have simply come to assess what is going on. I cannot repair and I do not have the tools to repair telephones."

"How long have you worked with the telephone company?" she asked.

"About eight years," he said. Betty went out of the office and shut the door. He heard the door being bolted. He hammered on the door and yelled, "I cannot repair your telephone!"

She said, "You are not leaving here until my telephones are repaired."

To which he replied, "I told you ma'am, I cannot repair telephones! I'm not paid to repair telephones. I'm not trained to repair telephones. I have no tools to repair telephones."

She said, "You told me that you have worked for the telephone company for eight years. They therefore must value you.

You get the telephones repaired." A few hours later, people arrived from the telephone company. All the telephones were repaired and the gentleman was let out of the office.

FESTINA LENTE (*HASTEN SLOWLY*)

I went to the opera. The chorus of the Houston Opera was sensational. Pearl said she'd miss me. Beryl said she'd miss me. Beryl said David was in love with me. Beryl said Ian was in love with me. I knew they were just hungry for good, sensible, normal people. I was hungry for good, sensible, normal people too.

Pearl and I went to another resale shop and I bought myself a stunning suit. It was on sale for $179 and reduced by 65 percent because no one else wanted it. There was then another 20 percent off because Pearl had a special card. In the end I bought it for $54. It is bright yellow with splashy black and white flowers on it. Fitted me perfectly.

We went to Brennan's for lunch, then to the Rothko Chapel—which was deadly, to say the least, with black paintings on the wall. The building was like a mausoleum. I had to get out. I didn't like it at all. We also went to see a domed painting on canvas. That was fascinating. Thirteenth-century and originally from Cypress, it had been cut up into pieces and sold. A fine philanthropic lady heard of its demise and employed about one hundred people to research and find all the pieces. It was restored in London. A very severe, purpose-built, domed building now housed these two Byzantine pieces. One of the Virgin and the Christ Child, and one of God the Father and God the Son.

Beryl cooked a wonderful dinner of rack of lamb and rice casserole, with great wine. Then off we went to see a movie. We were planning to see *The Heist*, but it was sold out, so we opted for *Training Day*. I had never seen such a violent movie. I do not like blood and guts. It was not scary—it was just violent. I asked David if that kind of thing does happen in real life, and he said that unfortunately it does. I have been separate from that kind of a life.

BUNG CAR

Monday, November 12. I called Fred to tell him I would be in Beaumont, Texas by quarter past eleven. I called Jenny in Natchez, to tell her I would be there by five or six. The air conditioning in my car was not working. The fan was on, but I had no air conditioning. Driving on 610-N, I headed toward 10-E, which would take me down into Beaumont, Texas. Bearing along 10-E from Beaumont on my way to Natchez, a very loud noise was coming through my open windows. The windows were open because of the bung air conditioner. While I had lunch with Fred and Melanie at their Crazy Ole restaurant, they sent my car to the Mercedes dealer to be checked. His computer told him that it was not my compressor and it was not my fan, so therefore it had to be the control panel. He could not repair it. Once I hit the road again, I called Fred to thank him for lunch, and he laughed and said, "I hope that Mercedes man told you that that's going to cost you about

$420. You will have to chew on that for a while. You need to get yourself some big pickles to chew on that!"

At 3:31 p.m. on Monday, November 12, I crossed the border from Texas into Louisiana. I didn't see a line, but I could see a sign that said, LOUISIANA WELCOME CENTER. This was my first time in Louisiana. The freeway was bordered by trees, green and dark red. The countryside was flat.

I heard better stories in Texas than I had heard anywhere except Australia. Folks topped each other, conversation after conversation. Miss Melanie told me that when oil was first found in Beaumont, Texas, in 1917—the gusher was giving out more oil per day than all of the rest of the United States put together. Exxon and Mobil and Gulf all began right there in Beaumont, Texas.

Fred showed me around his offices in Beaumont. Hundreds of photos of Fred with every famous person you could think of surrounded us. He drew my attention to a black and white photograph gifted to him by Bob Hope, a good friend. On one occasion when Fred was visiting Bob's home, he asked to use the restroom. Bob said, "I want you to use that restroom."

"Is there any particular reason why that restroom?" asked Fred.

"Yes," said Bob.

"What is it?" asked Fred.

"You'll see," said Bob.

"In I went and took a leak," said Fred, "and I came out laughing. This is what I saw." He picked up a photograph, clutched it proudly to his chest as though it was a treasured war medal, and said, "You know, when General Patton was leading the forces in the Second World War," he broke off momentarily and looked seriously and religiously committed to his country, "Patton said, 'When I get to the Nile I am going to piss in your river!' Now look at this Jillian," said Fred, and turned over the photograph with a flourish. There it was. Patton in full uniform. And yes, he was doing it. Fred laughed. "All Bob Hope asked was that I didn't copy it."

"How did you get it, though?" I asked.

"He sent it to me," said Fred.

I passed under a bridge with a sign that said VINTON–1 MILE. The sign looked as though it has been used for target practice. It was peppered with bullet holes. A casino on the river to the right was called Harrah's. I crossed the bridge over Lake Charles, Louisiana, headed onward and forward to Lafayette, then on to Baton Rouge, where I took the 110-N. It smelled different in that part of the South. It smelled swampy. With the windows down for lack of air conditioning, I could feel the humidity. I passed Eastwood Pentecostal Church, the first white-steepled church I had seen for a long time. Sam Houston played big in names as I traveled.

I passed a huge billboard announcing boldly that Bubba was running for office. I had heard people talk of a *Bubba*, a real Bubba, but I did not know that somebody would have that as their name.

A prime mover jiggled along in front of me. MACK, it said on the huge mudguards at the back. To the right of it was a truck carrying gasoline; its back was smart shiny stainless steel and shaped like one lens of a pair of stunning glasses. My car, and those for miles behind me, was reflected in its shining surface. The setting sun, gleaming off to the right, was also reflected. BENITO, it said. Sounded Italian.

A dark green camouflage bus tootled along to my right. It had four windows down each side and was the shape of a school bus. As I got closer to the back, I thought it said SCHOOL BUS until I recognized they had taken the *s* and the *h* away. COOL BUS, it said. She looked very hippy—with curtains made from bright yellow fabric smudged with flowers and garish flowers painted right across the front bumper bar. Someone with a great sense of humour dwelt within.

With the sun setting behind me I could see the light changing, even though it was only four thirty. I would not see Natchez in daylight. I passed a sign that said, La 91. I was still in Louisiana. Not *la* in capital letters but La, and then those figures 91. I wondered what in the world that was? La 91–2 MILES. It was a mystery to me. I passed a sign that said La 35–9 MILES. Of course! I was now in Louisiana, not Los Angeles.

Riding over a swamp with a name longer than I could read, I raced onto a bridge-like contraption, two lanes each way, separated, and dangling across the swamp. It looked like a swamp. It smelled like a swamp. It was a swamp. It said LAKE BEJO. It was a stinky little flat dark looking swamp with strange things poking out of it. The bridge went a long, long way. Another sign said, LAKE TALBA. It was not like any lake I had ever seen. I could see why people were afraid to go into these swamps. I felt afraid to even be driving over this one. I endeavored to pronounce the name of the swamp, river, lake—or whatever it was. Atchafalaya. Driving over the Mississippi River, I looked down on Baton Rouge, a beautiful-looking little city. I was about to take off onto the 110-N bound for Natchez, Mississippi.

WHICH BIG BRIDGE?

Wending my way out of Baton Rouge, I was on Highway 61-N, which gave me a choice: Scenic Route or Business District. I opted for Business District, thinking that at this time of night it would be a straight run through. But suddenly I was on route 190-W. I sure as hell didn't want to be going west, having been earnestly heading east for a month. Maybe 190-W and 61-N were the same. Stranger things have happened. But after driving ten miles, I didn't see 61-N pop up at all. I pulled into a gas station to discover that, oh yes—I did need to return back to the big bridge. "You remember coming over the big bridge?" said a huge gentleman who could hardly cope with lifting his eyes to help me. The whole scene reminded me of something out of the movie *Deliverance*. I did not remember a big bridge. How could I have missed a big bridge? "You know, *the big bridge*," he growled.

"How far back do I have to go?" I asked anxiously, thinking of Jenny and Ray and their dinner guests waiting.

"Didn't you just come over a big bridge?" my unhelpful helper asked accusingly.

"Oh yes," I said vaguely, remembering no big bridge.

"Well just past that," he said, "you look, and it will say Natchez."

"I saw two signs that said Natchez," I offered. "One said, TO 61-SCENIC ROUTE and one said, TO 61-BUSINESS DISTRICT. And then, miraculously, they melted away and became 190." He lowered his eyes and did not reply. He was done with me.

I filled the car with gas, turned it around, and headed back towards the mysterious big bridge. When I finally found it, I realized I had not come over it at all. The big bridge headed one way—east. But coming west you just went right along a little low road and under the big bridge. No wonder I didn't remember it. At least that was a relief. I was beginning to think I had lost something along the way on my trip.

Over the big bridge I found the little road sign 61-N and headed for Natchez, watching anxiously for the number 61 to pop up along the road. I passed a sign that said NATCHEZ–84 MILES. Eighty-four miles at fifty miles per hour; it was going to be a while before I found Jenny and Ray.

I passed a major power plant on my left. Not very beautiful, but the sight of Baton Rouge on the river at night was startlingly beautiful. There was something magic about the electric lights in the darkness. I wondered if there was less pollution in the air. It would be hard to imagine so, looking at the power plant. There was something that caused their electric lights to be much brighter than anything I ever remembered in LA. So Natchez, but later—much, much later than I had hoped.

I spent twenty anxious minutes careening along a beautifully surfaced road, which I hoped was Highway 61. Then I was careening along a not so beautifully surfaced road which I knew to be 61, when all of a sudden there was a fork and a tiny little sign that said 61 to the left. I careened left, hoping that I was headed north on 61, but the signs did not have the good manners to tell me. For twenty-one miles I had been looking for the first sign to reassure me I was still on 61. It still did not tell me whether it was north or south.

Another plane went down in Manhattan on November 12, 2001. Was I safer driving through the woods of Mississippi shrouded in a little fog? At least there were cars on the road. A few. I had been followed for miles by a one-eyed vehicle. I hoped he was not sussing me out. Nothing I could do but keep going. My doors were locked. Tires were good. I was gassed up. Telephone was at the ready. God send angels. I was late for dinner, but as Casey said, "They'll wait for you, you are worth it."

NATCHEZ

The Akubra and my pale-blue tracksuit had to be my dress for Jenny's dinner, or I would be embarrassingly late. I took a deep breath and "arrived." Spectacular home, gracious and sophisticated company, good wine and delicious food—and I soon forgot my anxiety over being lost in the woods.

I had been talking with Trevor from time to time on my journey. Over lunch the next day, as Jenny and I were doing a quick catch up I started in, "I've been talking to…." No name was mentioned.

Jenny, ever the gentlest of gracious ladies, leaned in over the table until her face was almost touching mine to announce in a whisper, "You are going to marry this man!" How unexpected. Confronting. No name had been mentioned. No detail at all. What she placed on the plate in front of me with her words was startlingly similar to what David had told me before I left California, with Nicholas adding that, at my age I needed to marry someone with a similar background, as we did not have time to get to know each other.

"When we need to argue or fight, we go to a restaurant," he told me. "Then we are compelled to be polite."

Later, driving up the curved driveway to Longwood mansion in Natchez, I had goose bumps. Magnificent trees line the path, autumn-colored, reaching up to the sky. An octagonal mansion whose construction was begun with great joy in the 1860s for a cotton baron by the name of Dr. Haller Nutt. Stunning outside, the façade was completed, but the interior was not. War was declared. The Civil War. The workmen left to join Lincoln's army and never came back. Only the basement had been completed. The family finally abandoned it in 1930, never having been able to finish it. It was amazing and sad all at the same time. Under the trees, Spanish moss draped and folded into the morning mist.

I was headed for Destin, Florida. It was November 13. I had left California on October 17. Over the bridge I went, over the river and back into Louisiana. Five miles from Jenny and Ray's, on this side of the river and that side of the river, the Civil War was fought. The main street of Vidalia, Louisiana, displayed little drawings of the paddle steamers which had plied this river for years. Miss-Lou. Mississippi-Louisiana. Another border.

YOU START FROM HERE

There is something unsettling about starting off in the wrong direction. I spent thirty minutes trying to understand why I was on 94-W when I really wanted to be on 94-E. I stopped at a gas station and spoke to a big, young, southern man who helped me. "You just want to get right over there, just right over the bridge. You turn right there. You be right. You go right that way." He was strong, in the way of one of those people you think could be a fireman, a policeman, a father, and a construction worker all in together, but sure would make you feel safe.

I turned around and went back to exactly where I started from. That was the message. Luke chided me once when he was very little and I was very lost. I had blubbered, "I don't know where to start from."

He looked at me seriously with his velvet-brown eyes and said, "Mummy, you start right here."

I passed a long, low, black-painted building with some orange decorations in the window, sporting an enormous orange sign, which shouted, LIVE NUDE GIRLS. Does that mean there's a possibility of dead nude girls?

The trees I passed were full of golden autumn mixed with a few darkly garbed pines. Coming toward me on the opposite side of the road was a man—walking, pushing a small machine. His job was to mark the line down the middle of the road. Manually. He was followed by a truck with lights flashing. I thought lines were drawn by a truck, but he was walking and his small machine was painting. The truck was happily following and flashing.

Tuesday afternoon and I drove on 98-E towards McComb—logging country, fragrant with the smell of newly cut timber. Timber yards punctured the sides of the road. I stopped to get a bottle of water at a small gas station before I headed onto 55-S. The owner of the gas station was an East Indian. Whatever had brought him to that little gas station in a southern corner of the US, he had certainly found a cash cow. In the few minutes I was inside paying my bill, there must have been twenty persons in and out, all purchasing. Another story to ponder.

GUIDING ME

I was sixty miles west of Mobile, Alabama, when Griff called, wanting to know my whereabouts. "Good," he said, "now I have some idea of your arrival time." He was about to scurry off to a small event for the Sacred Heart Hospital. My hospital.

I stopped for gas after our conversation. "Have you eaten?" he had asked me.

"Well, yes," I had said, "I had cookies and water." The cookies were two peanut butter, and two oatmeal and raisin. They were utterly indistinguishable one from the other, pertly wrapped packages of Grandma's Special, and the best I could find at the last pit stop. I had been determined to find something nourishing and fresh. The hot food all looked a day or two old. The chicken was encrusted with breadcrumbs from the Second World War. A sausage or saveloy of some kind, rolling fitfully around on metal rollers to keep it warm, was the last surviving remnant of the British Empire. Bangers, but no mash. Shelf after shelf of candy, ice cream, sweet cookies. The best I could buy was what is called a Slim Jim, a little package with a stick of cheese and a stick of beef jerky. I opened it in a desperate bid for protein. The cheese was dreadful. I could not bear to approach the beef jerky.

At five past seven I crossed into Alabama. WELCOME TO BEAUTIFUL ALABAMA, a sign said, immediately preceding a sign on the side of the road that said, END OF MOTOR AID CALL BOXES. There had to be a reason for this. Did they not expect motorists to need aid in Alabama? I had been into Mobile, Alabama, once before. I flew in from Los Angeles, headed for Destin to attend a special dinner. I flew first into Dallas, where I was stuck for seven hours while the air flight controllers watched the threatening weather, so I sat over a glass of wine or two discussing life with a gentleman who was also waiting to fly into Mobile, Alabama. I had planned this route to save a little money. I would rent a car from Mobile Rent-a-Car and drive the few hours to Destin, Florida. Maybe it saved money, but I missed the dinner. This was now my second visit. I was nearly into Mobile. It was five past seven, with about a two-and-a-half-hour driving time to Griff's.

Headed for Florida and a brand-new home, I felt good. I

also felt a little frightened. I did not want to get stuck. I wanted to give way to the adventure of Destin and Griff's gracious welcome of me.

At 8:00 p.m. I crossed the Florida state line. At this point I felt like a heroine—in my own eyes, at least. I was supremely pleased with myself and full of my own sense of self-importance. The urge to show off was strong. I had driven by myself from the West Coast to the East of the US—from California to Florida. Maybe I would start a club for older single women who have made such a journey. I did it! I arrived at the front of Griff's home at a quarter to ten, having driven myself all the way across the US.

A WELL-KNOWN STRANGER

Once upon a time, I had a fine American friend who fell in love with and married a Parisian girl. Not a French girl—a Parisian. He moved from Washington, DC to live with his bride in Paris. She was beautiful in the slim way that some such women can be, and daringly chic in her dress. And she had a babe. Every now and again I would catch her looking at the child in her arms in utter astonishment, as though trying to comprehend where such a child had come from and why it had been placed in her arms. She managed to look both puzzled and aghast.

This most elegant of young ladies and her husband had been kind enough to offer me a bed for a few nights in their mid-Paris apartment. It suited me very well. I am not sure how well it suited her.

One day, she quietly approached to tell me that her parents were coming to visit. I exclaimed over how lovely that would be for her, for them, and for the babe, as well as for her husband. She was quiet for a minute. Thoughtful. "Yes," she said with some hesitation. "I think that will be all right. I think they do not mind foreigners."

Foreigners? Me? A foreigner? I had not thought of myself as a foreigner. If I thought hard about it, I would have considered I was a regular Aussie girl visiting Paris alone, happy to be in good company. A foreigner indeed! I felt a little miffed—even affronted. I reflected on my huffiness in the face of possible rejection by people who knew not a thing about me, and I remembered another incident or two that had provoked a similar feeling of effrontery at other times in other places.

In the years I lived in Chicago I had been confronted with the alienating fact that there were rather large notices pinned boldly to the walls of every police station I ever passed informing me in no uncertain terms that I was required to register twice a year because I was an alien. An alien indeed! Who did they think they were, to call me an alien? I was a good Aussie girl after all. Normal in every way. At least up until then.

There were a lot of police stations in Chicago, hence a lot of notices with their big fingers pointing right at me. It was confronting and affronting, and unavoidable. There were forms to fill out and finger prints to be taken. I was well and truly labeled. I was now officially a Resident Alien. It did not feel comfortable.

I lived for a year in the notorious witch city of Salem, Massachusetts. In conversation with a neighbor, and in what turned out to be a misguided attempt to be friendly, I asked him—had he ever traveled. "Oh yes," he replied, eyes sparkling. He pointed over his shoulder, and with a backwards nod of his head and a proud toss of glossy black locks, he said, "I've been to Lynne." Not knowing that name, and unsure of which country it was in, I smiled inanely and told him that was wonderful. "Oh yes, wonderful!" he replied, grinning with pleasure.

It took me a day or two of detective work to discover the location of Lynne. It was the suburb right next to Salem. Then it was my turn, once more, to really feel a stranger. We were living on different pages.

Maurice Chevalier—French, elegant, charming, and musical. I was beguiled by his accent, or perhaps he was beguiling when he sang that lovely song, "I Remember It Well." I laugh still as I observe in my many lives how poignant and true are those words he sang to me so many years ago. He remembered special moments of the heart—where they had been, how he had felt, what had happened, the color of her dress. He remembered it well indeed.

She remembered too, all the details, where they had been, how she had felt, what had happened. All of it. But what he remembered and what she remembered did not match. They were not congruent. Despite each being sure that they were correct in every detail, they were not on the same page. They were not singing from the same song sheet.

Now, as I sat down to dinner with Griff I was carrying a

song sheet in hand, and I had to sing a little song to Griff. He who was so delighted that I was coming to stay with him. He who had gone out of his way to prepare. He who offered me a place to relax and recover and start my next new life. He who said I could stay until I found a place of my own. He who had offered me years of generosity. I had to show him a one-inch-square photo of Trevor. I turned the paper to Griff. Tears began to roll down his cheeks. "You are going to marry this man," he whispered.

SURPRISE IN A PAPER BAG

Trevor told me that he had worn blue suede shoes on the one and only date we had. I do not remember that. He told me that Willis was watching through the kitchen window when he kissed me goodnight on the cheek. I do not remember that either. Although I do remember that it was the wont of Willis to greet any date of mine at the door with, "Are you the same one who was here last night?" leaving me blushing with mortification.

I do remember that he was wearing a beautiful, pale-blue, wool sports jacket. He says it was white. I also remember his smooth skin, healthy and glowing in the half-light. We both remember that we traveled the nine miles to and from the city of Melbourne by train. What we did in the city neither of us remember, although we agree that it would have been charmingly innocent. We both remember that we walked the mile from the station back to my parents' home in East Malvern, as neither of us was old enough to drive a car. Trevor has told me since that he was very keen to date girls who were older than he because there was a chance they would have a car that he could drive.

He remembers singing to himself on his lonely walk back to the station. And he does not sing. Pleased with himself he was.

That was it. We moved into different orbits, different countries, different friends, different lives. I met his bride only once. Beautiful she was, in a sweetly innocent kind of way. He did not ever meet my groom.

Decades later, when we had resumed contact, I had sent him a black and white photocopy of a photograph of me, A4-size, with MEMORIES scribbled across it. In return he had sent a photograph of himself. A joyful photograph, also on A4, but placed right in the middle of the page, it was a tiny, one-inch square. It was this photograph that I turned to Griff.

"I will wear a pumpkin-colored shirt so that you will recognize me," Trevor offered when I told him I would be flying into Melbourne from Florida for a few days, on vacation provided by Luke and Toby.

"He's threatening to wear a pumpkin-colored shirt?" I thought. How could I have known that a man I had not seen for forty years, now courageous enough to wear a pumpkin-colored shirt in public, would walk into Melbourne airport carrying arms full of surprises just for me? "I will recognize you," I said. I did.

I had asked my boys what I should wear to meet this man I had not seen for forty years. Luke, his wife Melissa, and Toby and me were trekking up the side of a mountain in Tasmania at the time. They looked me over thoughtfully. "What you are wearing now will be fine, Mum," they said. Boys!

Trevor told me later that I looked very Californian when I stepped off the plane. I thought I looked normal. In his kitchen in Melbourne he turned to me, "Champagne?" he asked.

"Yes," I said. "I would like that."

He proposed the next day.

MELBOURNE TOWN

And now here I was, returned to live in Melbourne. I left when I was twenty-two years old, planning to be gone for a year. But life overwhelmed my best-laid plans, and I was fifty-nine years old when I returned. I was much changed. Melbourne was much changed. Most of my friends were much changed. I had been a stranger in a foreign land many times since I had left. Now I was a stranger in a foreign land again.

A NEW PAPER BAG

Here I will find a new paper bag. I will hold it to my mouth and remind myself to breathe in and out. I will find one in which to place gentle offerings of love.

And if I am blessed again with good fortune, I will find a paper bag at my door step—filled with gentle, thoughtful, caring wisdom; good humour; and loving encouragement.

ACKNOWLEDGMENTS

Many folk encouraged me to write in the years I was resident in California. I thank them all. Some persisted by gifting me with beautiful volumes, each with hearty paper and empty pages, awaiting my dab hand. Large and small, these books have an array of covers: wooden, embellished and embroidered. Special gifts all, they urged me to pick up my pen.

When I met Bob Danzig in California in 1998, how could I have imagined the role he would play in the birthing of this book? He had retired from his role as Vice President, The Hearst Corporation, and General Manager of Newspapers only a week before we met, and had written requesting assistance with the wide dissemination of his book, Angel Threads. I was able to arrange the public interview he requested. We lunched at the Four Seasons. He followed with a letter of appreciation and we corresponded a little. I kept those measures of his thoughtfulness.

Then came 9/11, which caused me to choose to drive solo from California to Florida, dictating glimpses of that adventure. Some time later I wrote asking if Bob would be able to meet with my son Toby and me when we visited New York. He graciously gave us time, as he did when I returned to New York with Mr. T.

Settled back in Australia, and dipping my toe in the edge of the wide ocean of the writing world, I contacted Bob for comment. He offered warm encouragement, along with the name of his publisher, Kira Rosner. Angel Threads were at work. Through Kira and her encouragement I met Paul Cohen of Monkfish Book Publishing Company, who continued the encouragement. And then Colin Rolfe whose hand guided this book through the design process.

Bob has left this mortal coil, and I miss him, he was and is, a person to miss. Kira, Paul, Colin and I have communicated across the ether from Melbourne, Australia to New York during this torrid time of Covid-19. The two piercing events of 9/11 and the Covid-19 pandemic have threaded their way through the birthing process of this book, and marked us all.

My sons, Luke Benjamin and Toby John have encouraged me all the way. Mr. T has been by my side to encourage and comment every step of the way. Every friend who knows of the project has offered warm encouragment. I am grateful.

SATURDAY
HARVARD CLUB
44th ST / NOON
IN LOBBY
Then walk to
CATS - 2:30p
SAT MATINEE
Sept 25th
DANZIG

Dear Jillian —
*Always **choose** to **lead** your life!*

A treat to visit with you and your impressive son, Toby. I hope you find pleasure in the enclosed CD. Every good wish!

Bob Danzig

VITAMINS for the SPIRIT

Have five "BE" attitudes

1. Be able to –
   Separate yourself from the crowd.
2. Be able to –
   Live in day tight compartments.
3. Be able to –
   Go the extra mile.
4. Be able to –
   Find instruction in adversity.
5. Be able to –
   Never let anyone rain on your parade.

Bob Danzig

Hearst Newspapers

VITAMINS for the SPIRIT

Welcome Every Morning With a Smile

Look on the new day as another special gift, another golden opportunity to complete what you were unable to finish yesterday. Be a self-starter. Let your first hour set the theme of success and positive action that is certain to echo through your entire day. Today will never happen again. Don't waste it with a false start or no start at all. You were not born to fail.

Bob Danzig

Hearst Newspapers

www.ingramcontent.com/pod-product-compliance
Lightning Source LLC
LaVergne TN
LVHW051836080426
835512LV00018B/2909